T0358258

Cambridge Elements ≡

Elements in Public and Nonprofit Administration
edited by
Andrew Whitford
University of Georgia
Robert Christensen
Brigham Young University

CAN GOVERNANCE BE INTELLIGENT?

An Interdisciplinary Approach and Evolutionary Modeling for Intelligent Governance in the Digital Age

Eran Vigoda-Gadot
University of Haifa
HSE-National Research University

Shaftesbury Road, Cambridge CB2 8EA, United Kingdom

One Liberty Plaza, 20th Floor, New York, NY 10006, USA

477 Williamstown Road, Port Melbourne, VIC 3207, Australia

314–321, 3rd Floor, Plot 3, Splendor Forum, Jasola District Centre, New Delhi – 110025, India

103 Penang Road, #05–06/07, Visioncrest Commercial, Singapore 238467

Cambridge University Press is part of Cambridge University Press & Assessment, a department of the University of Cambridge.

We share the University's mission to contribute to society through the pursuit of education, learning and research at the highest international levels of excellence.

www.cambridge.org
Information on this title: www.cambridge.org/9781009475884

DOI: 10.1017/9781009437783

First published 2024

A catalogue record for this publication is available from the British Library.

ISBN 978-1-009-47588-4 Hardback
ISBN 978-1-009-43776-9 Paperback
ISSN 2515-4303 (online)
ISSN 2515-429X (print)

Can Governance be Intelligent?

An Interdisciplinary Approach and Evolutionary Modeling for Intelligent Governance in the Digital Age

Elements in Public and Nonprofit Administration

DOI: 10.1017/9781009437783
First published online: May 2024

Eran Vigoda-Gadot
University of Haifa
HSE-National Research University
Author for correspondence: Eran Vigoda-Gadot, eranv@poli.haifa.ac.il

Abstract: Intelligence is a concept that occurs in multiple contexts and has various meanings. It refers to the ability of human beings and other entities to think and understand the world around us. It represents a set of skills directed at problem-solving and targeted at producing effective results. Thus, intelligence and governance are an odd couple. We expect governments and other governing institutions to operate in an intelligent manner, but too frequently we criticize their understanding of serious public problems, their decisions, behaviors, managerial skills, ability to solve urgent problems, and overall governability wisdom. This Element deals with such questions using interdisciplinary insights (i.e., psychological, social, institutional, biological, technological) on intelligence and integrating it with knowledge in governance, administration, and management in public and nonprofit sectors. This Element proposes the IntelliGov framework, that may extend both our theoretical, methodological, analytical, and applied understanding of intelligent governance in the digital age.

This Element also has a video abstract: www.cambridge.org/EPNP-Gadot

Keywords: intelligence, governance and public administration, digital era, interdisciplinarity, public interest

ISBNs: 9781009475884 (HB), 9781009437769 (PB), 9781009437783 (OC)
ISSNs: 2515-4303 (online), 2515-429X (print)

Contents

1 Introduction: The Intelligent Us   2

2 Intelligence: Conceptual and Theoretical Background   5

3 Is There Multiple Intelligence in Governance?   10

4 Multiple Intelligence: An Interdisciplinary Perspective   11

5 Toward Intelligent Governance: An Evolutionary Model   16

6 IntelliGov: A Comprehensive Interdisciplinary Model of Governance Intelligence   31

7 IntelliGov in the Digital Age: How Technology Revolutionize Governance Intelligence   34

8 Future Studies on Intelligent Governance: Major Challenges   47

9 Discussion: Toward a Theory of Multiple Intelligence in Governance   54

10 Summary: Can Governance Be Intelligent, and How?   61

References   64

Prologue

This Element looks at governance as potentially capable of becoming more intelligent and closer to its mission of better serving citizens and effectively promoting public values. It is inspired by a rich set of interdisciplinary perspectives exploring the meaning of intelligence for individuals, institutions, and computerized systems of the digital era. Building on knowledge acquired over more than a century by psychologists, sociologists, economists, political scientists, administrative and policy experts, information and computer system scholars, we try to explain why and how intelligence, both as an idea and as a practice, is relevant for governance. In other words, we argue that governance may become intelligent.

To do so, we explore the meaning and various layers of intelligence, and further relate governance intelligence with the goal of serving citizens as end-users. We maintain that turning government and governance into more intelligent bodies of policy formators and decision-makers it is first essential to use a solid theoretical framework that provides essential building blocks for thematic and analytical progress. Such a framework must integrate knowledge about intelligence from as many reliable sources as possible and use it to suggest explanatory/analytic rules alongside practical pathways. Therefore, the Element progresses over several phases. We begin by a conceptual and theoretical discussion, move to exploratory mapping of existing studies on intelligence, and finally suggest explanatory modelling which strive to lead to a comprehensive and integrative IntelliGov model.

Two major groups of readers are targeted – academics and practitioners – mainly those dealing with the business of government, administration, and policymaking. We believe that most of the sections are relevant to individuals from both groups. The Element is aimed primarily at scholars of public administration, business management, political science, and of other social sciences interested in the nexus between governance, management, psychology, sociology, technology, and data science. For academics and researchers much benefit is in the interdisciplinary orientation of the writing, in reviewing conceptual and theoretical ideas on the meaning of intelligence in general and more specifically, for governance. The models developed throughout the Element are also gradually extending academic inspiration by carefully tailoring knowledge about intelligence from different perspectives and aiming to testable propositions that can be used in future empirical studies. Such empirical directions will help advance explanatory studies on characteristics of and antecedents to intelligent governance. We believe it will also advance knowledge on potential outcomes of intelligent governance in terms of decision-making and policies.

The Element is also targeted at readers with practical orientations. These may include politicians, public administrators, individuals from the voluntary and nonprofit sector, active citizens, and other partners of government – those who share the burden of making our nations run in a more intelligent way. That is why we believe that CEOs of the business and not-for-profit sectors should also be interested in this Element. These individuals who constitute the managerial elite of our societies also carry the responsibility to advance knowledge and intelligence in and around government halls, vis-à-vis the bureaucratic code of action in the public sector. Finally, we hope that citizens themselves may also find the Element enlightening and contributory to the formation of intelligent-based communities that work closely with formal authorities in governance while directly influencing the quality of life of as many as possible.

Taken altogether, the general intellectual message of the Element is that governance can be intelligent but the road toward such an aim is long and complex. To bring governance closer to its goal of greater intelligence, theoretical pieces of the scientific puzzle must be well integrated, combined systematically, and clearly presented to the readers. We hope the next sections will meet these ambitious goals.

1 Introduction: The Intelligent Us

Intelligence is a concept that occurs in multiple contexts and has various meanings. It refers to the ability of human beings and other entities to think and understand the world around us. It represents a set of skills directed at problem solving and targeted at producing effective results. When these results are relevant for public spheres and policies, intelligence becomes relevant for governance. Studies on intelligence come from different sources, use various disciplinary perspectives, tools, and methods, and focus on goals at the individual, organizational, and general societal levels. They all seek a better understanding of intelligence as a tool for moving humankind toward modernity, progress, and prosperity.

In recent decades, intelligence with regard to governance has gained a special meaning, with the rise of artificial, technological, and digital capabilities that have dramatically increased the flow and use of data and information in all public sector and governing spheres. Whereas previously, knowledge about intelligence relied mainly on the ability of humans and institutions to solve public problems, a new digital player has redefined the boundaries of intelligence. Hence, a comprehensive understanding of intelligence in governance must consider the integration of human, institutional, and more profoundly, digital machine minds. This combination will become a powerful factor in changing the world around us. We have not even begun to study or understand this development fully from a theoretical or practical perspective. Its potential contribution to public administration, governance, and overall human progress is of major significance.

Mankind is perhaps one of the more intelligent species on earth, some say *the* most intelligent among all others. Has it managed to make its governing bodies, political institutions, and public administration systems intelligent as well? In other words, can governance be intelligent? If "Government is us" (King & Stivers, 1998), is there an intelligent us in the realm of states, nations, and communities? How can governing institutions and individuals working around them become more intelligent? And what impact do they have on our life, on the public interest, and on society? These questions, in many ways and variants, have been at the center of theoretical and empirical debate in public administration and governance for decades. They were approached by scholars with a variety of scientific perspectives, experience, and skills. The debate has resulted with rich and diverse conceptual frameworks, but practically with no clear say on governance as intelligent systems.

The terms "good government," "sound governance," "smart government," "new and learning governance" were all used in a handful of studies over the years, and especially since the beginning of the millennia (e.g., Crozier, 2008; Rotberg, 2014; Meijer & Bolivar, 2016; Grossi et al., 2020; Preira et al., 2018, to name only few). These and many other studies improve our understanding of the meaning of intelligence in the context of governance. They undoubtedly revealed at least some of the ambiguities involved in the meaning of intelligence, suggesting that it relates to the learning, knowledge, talents, values, skills, adaptation, and productivity of those involved in the hardcore of policymaking. As such, intelligence has been deemed necessary for those involved in leading complex public institutions. Nevertheless, while we still build on such past terminologies, we look at intelligent governance as the integration of concepts and ideas. We suggest that the terms used to describe governance such as good, sound, smart, and new can all be combined and create the concept of intelligent governance. This concept aligns with those described above. However, it also describes a form of governance that is faster, broader, fairer, and more equal in terms of moral values and the fair distribution of resources for better problem solving.

Nevertheless, epistemological consensus about the existence and relevance of intelligent governance per se, not to mention methodological and empirical knowledge about its meaning, measurement, and analysis is still far from complete. If intelligence is at the heart of our analytical thinking and practical decisions in governance, it deserves systematic consideration. This should include more comprehensive coverage in theory, in explanatory models, in methodological frameworks, and in in-depth ambitious analytical and empirical field studies. An intellectual and empirical effort may advance the field and open new roads for both thinkers and makers of future policies. The prime goal of this Element is therefore to suggest new perspectives for discussion at both the abstractive and applied levels. We aim at extending the dynamic general discussion about human and nonhuman intelligence into the explicit territories of governance, public administration, public management, and political science.

Without doubt, intelligence is a concept with multidisciplinary contexts and with various meanings. Studies deal with conventional biological/human and nonhuman intelligence (e.g., Coren, 1995; Trewaves, 2005; Roth, 2015; Hedlund, 2020), emotional intelligence (e.g., Salovey & Mayer, 1990), social intelligence (e.g., Goleman, 2006), institutional-organizational and business intelligence (e.g., Talaoui & Kohtamaki, 2021), collective and cultural Intelligence (e.g., Ott & Michailova, 2018), artificial intelligence (e.g., Glikson & Woolley, 2020) and related aspects of deep learning and human–machine interactions for combined HMI intelligence (e.g., Gonçalves et al., 2019). Still, not much has been explored and written on the integrative and interdisciplinary meaning of intelligence for public administration, public services, public policy, and governance. Are these studies, and others, speak about the same topic but only in different languages? Or are they referring to different meanings of the same phenomena?

The questions stemming from such observation are many. Can governing institutions such as public administration organizations and other public service and nonprofit agencies be more, or less, intelligent? Is there a specific intelligent type of public service that makes some sorts of governance more intelligent than others? What ideas and theories may be useful in forming our understanding about governance intelligence and in building such intelligence in practice? Can we point to a more effective type of intelligent governance with local and global implications? What disciplinary sources of knowledge are needed for building this model? And finally, how can we comprehensively use knowledge about humans, emotions, institutions, machines, and computers to foster better public services, policies, and decisions in governance?

This Element is aimed at dealing with such questions. We modestly admit that we may not be able to provide convincing answers to all questions. But we will make a thorough effort to uncover some of the core issues related with intelligent governance. Toward this goal, we basically treat intelligent governance as a combination of human intelligence, institutional intelligence, and artificial intelligence for better use of information, data, knowledge, and technology to improve the effectiveness and efficiency of government, its management, decision-making, and policymaking. Thus, we argue that better understanding of the meaning of intelligence in governance must build on interdisciplinary ground. This can be done by employing new psychological and social insights, together with modern digital terminologies and concepts. These may lead to use of more innovative theoretical modeling, and most importantly by integrating them comprehensively. By looking into intelligent governance from a multiple disciplinary lens and by adopting multi-levels of analysis, we hope to break new ground for more coherent theory in this understudied and overlooked field.

Our prime goal is thus threefold: (1) to advance interdisciplinary theory on the meaning of intelligence and its contribution to understanding governance in the digital age, (2) to suggest a set of evolutionary models for intelligence governance, which eventually lead to a comprehensive IntelliGov model, and (3) to demonstrate the model's theoretical and applied contribution for public administration, public management, and public policy of the future, especially in the digital era when intelligence of machines compete with intelligence of humans and become substantial in all territories of governance.

2 Intelligence: Conceptual and Theoretical Background

2.1 The Meaning of Intelligence

Intellect is the ability to think and understand the world around us. Therefore, intelligence is commonly inferred to humans who use intellect for various purposes in our world. Nonetheless, intelligence may have similar meaning for nonhumans, to machines and algorithms, and to abstract players such as social and organizational entities that hold the capacity to learn, understand, and develop ideas and processes.

The meaning of intelligence derives from the Latin nouns *intelligentia* or *intellēctus*, which stem from the verb *intelligere* (to comprehend or perceive). However, there is no clear definition for intelligence (Sternberg & Detterman, 1986) and its controversy rests in disagreements among scientists about what abilities it captures and whether it is quantifiable (Legg & Hutter, 2007a, 2007b). Following Richard Herrnstein and Charles Murray's (1994) influential work on *The Bell Curve* of intelligence a group of scientists published on December 13, 1994 an op-ed in the Wall street Journal titled *"Mainstream Science on Intelligence."* Fifty-two scientists who signed the letter set out twenty-five numbered conclusions on mainstream agreements among researchers on intelligence which are fully described in the major textbooks, professional journals, and encyclopedias in intelligence (Neisser et al., 1996; Gottfredson, 1997). However, and almost 30 years later, there is still no consensus among scientists about the full meaning of intelligence. A careful yet only partial selection of definitions mention (1) Judgment, otherwise called "good sense," "practical sense," "initiative," the faculty of adapting one's self to circumstances ... auto-critique (Binet, 1905, 1916a); (2) The aggregate or global capacity of the individual to act purposefully, to think rationally, and to deal effectively with his environment (Wechsler, 1944); (3) The ability to deal with cognitive complexity (Gottfredson, 1998); and (4) Goal-directed adaptive behavior (Sternberg & Salter, 1982).

More recently and based on a synthesis of more than seventy definitions from psychology, philosophy, and computer science, Legg and Hutter (2007a) suggested that "Intelligence measures an agent's ability to achieve goals in a wide range of environments." This definition has also been mathematically formalized (Legg & Hutter, 2007b). It represents a general mental capability that, among other things, involves the ability to reason, plan, solve problems, think abstractly, comprehend complex ideas, learn quickly, and learn from experience. It reflects a broader and deeper capability for comprehending our surroundings – "catching on," "making sense" of things, or "figuring out" what to do (Gottfredson, 1997). One of the more discussed definitions over the years was suggested by Gardner (1983). In his view intelligence represents a set of skills directed at problem solving, enabling individuals to resolve genuine problems or difficulties that he or she encounters and, when appropriate, to create an effective product. It must also entail the potential for finding or creating problems and thereby laying the groundwork for the acquisition of new knowledge. Hence, psychologists agree that individuals differ from one another in their ability to understand complex ideas, to adapt effectively to the environment, to learn from experience, to engage in various forms of reasoning, to overcome obstacles by taking thought. Intellectual performance will vary based on occasions, different domains, and as judged by different criteria.

The meaning of intelligence thus benefited from a variety of perspectives and definitions, many of them developed and suggested by psychologists, which stimulated studies in many disciplines such as social and exact sciences, natural science, management, business, organizational science, digital and technology. In the next section, we review the evolution of these studies at glance, to demonstrate the progress that has been made over almost a century, and to try and use it for our purposes in studying governance intelligence.

2.2 Evolution of Intelligence Studies at Glance

Early theories of intelligence focused on the human and individual level and were evoked with the psychometric approach introduced by Alfred Binet and colleagues at the beginning of the twentieth century (Wasserman, 2018). Rather than focus on humans' learned information such as math and reading, Binet and Simon (1916) focused on other mental abilities of individuals such as attention and memory and suggested a series of tests designed to assess mental abilities (Binet, 1916). The scale they developed became known as the Binet-Simon Intelligence scale. It was later developed into the Stanford-Binet scale (Terman & Merill, 1937). Today, Binet is often cited as one of the most influential psychologists in history thanks to his studies which serve as the basis for modern intelligence tests (IQ – Intelligence Quotient; Binet, 1916a and Stern, 1914) and for other theories on nonhuman intelligence.

Another cluster of intelligence theories, still at the human level, stem from the educational and developmental progressing approach such as Piaget (1972) and Vygotsky (1978). By observing children, these theories suggested that intelligence develops by a continuous assimilation of new information with existing cognitive structures of individuals. This line of thinking was followed by Howard Gardner's seminal work, *Frame of Mind* (1983), which was influenced by the works of Binet (1916) and Stern (1914). Within his paradigm of human intelligence, Gardner defines it as being "the ability to learn" or "to solve problems," referring to intelligence as a "bio-psychological potential to process information" (Steinberg, 1989). Sternberg (1985) also suggested the triarchic theory with three core aspects of intelligence: analytic, creative, and practical. These aspects refer to the abilities of the human mind/brain and they need to be in balance. Analytic (or academic) intelligence received more attention in early years of study. Thus, they also gained more empirical and methodological support with measurable tools of IQ (e.g., Kovacs & Conway, 2019).

Only in recent decades more attention is given to creative and practical intelligence. This process has derived from the rise of neuroscience, and studies suggested ways to measure creative intelligence (e.g., Simonton, 2012) and practical/tacit intelligence (e.g., Hedlund, 2020). It was further suggested that types of human intelligence may diverge across cultures (e.g., Heath, 1983) mainly due to language and conceptual differences and due to experience of subjects with the world around them. Cultural differences remain a major challenge to studying intelligence even today. Its relevance to governance is clear as nations differ in types of their bureaucratic systems, organizational culture, managerial culture, and overall social values. Thus, the role of human intelligence in and around those systems may be subject to cultural bias and must be considered. This idea will be discussed later, especially in view of the digital era which is presumed by some studies to decrease cultural gaps among nations in many ways. Thus, recent studies have further discussed the concept of cultural intelligence (e.g., Ott & Michailova, 2018), highlighting its significance in various fields such as management, business, education, and network analysis.

Finally, studies theoretically suggested and empirically examined nonhuman intelligence among other living species such as animals and even plants. Attention has been given to mental abilities and comparing them between species. As language is a brier in such cases, studies used measures of problem solving, social abilities, numerical and verbal reasoning abilities. Major challenges in this area are consensual definitions and operationalization of intelligence across species and contexts (e.g., Kohler, 1925; on the intelligence of apes and Coren, 1995; on the intelligence of dogs). Other studies focused on the intelligence of chimpanzees, dolphins, elephants, parrots, rats, mammals, birds, reptiles, and fish (e.g., Roth, 2015). Evidence of a general factor (g-Factor) of intelligence has been observed in nonhuman animals.[1] It has been argued that plants should also be classified as intelligent based on their ability to sense and model external and internal environments. They arc intelligent to the level that they adjust their morphology, physiology, and phenotype accordingly to ensure self-preservation and reproduction (e.g., Trewaves, 2005). Plants are not limited to automated sensory-motor responses; however, they can discriminate positive and negative experiences and of "learning" (registering memories) from their past experiences. They are also capable of communication, accurately computing their circumstances, using sophisticated cost–benefit analysis and taking tightly controlled actions to mitigate and control the diverse environmental stressors (Rensing et al., 2009). Thus, biological theorists of intelligence contribute unique aspects of this filed, building on brain and neuroscience to explain where intelligence is structured in our brains and what may explain its formation and development over time, space, and ecosystems (e.g., Wahlsten, 2002). Hence, biological intelligence studies are at the core of human and other living species intelligence research, whereas artificial intelligence (AI) is, by definition, nonhuman related. In addition, studies on the relationship between biology/human and machine/nonhuman intelligence are emerging in recent years, especially with greater understanding of Human–Machine Interaction (HMI). All these forms and crossroads of intelligence may turn to be relevant to governance as well. Understanding the mechanisms leading to greater intelligence among humans and nonhumans may shade light on intelligence of more abstractive entities like governance and public administrative systems. Inferring from biological nonhumans to such entities may be argued to be indirect and

---

[1] *g* Factor (General factor of intelligence), is a psychometric construct that summarizes the correlations observed between an individual's scores on a wide range of cognitive abilities. First described in humans, the *g* factor has since been identified in a number of nonhuman species. Cognitive ability and intelligence cannot be measured using the same, largely verbally dependent, scales developed for humans. Instead, intelligence is measured using a variety of interactive and observational tools focusing on innovation, habit reversal, social learning, and responses to novelty.

less trivial, but it is undoubtedly stimulating research within the scope of better capturing the entire meaning of intelligence in governance. Thus, it will be discussed more extensively later, with the exploration of our evolutionary model for intelligence in government.

2.3 Origins of Multiple Intelligence among Humans

Over more than a century of studies, knowledge and understanding of intelligence evolved and changed from an anchored/fixed approach to a floating/ multiple approach that inspired developments in this field. Traditionally, scientists agreed that intelligence is pre-determined by genes and fixed in our brains from the day we are born. The fixed-biological orientation treated intelligence as largely predetermined in peoples' genes. As such, it was suggested that humans cannot increase their intelligence significantly or, if at all, change it only marginally (e.g., Detterman & Sternberg, 1982; Remsden et al., 2011). The alternative approach of floating/multiple intelligence suggested that, despite some fixed elements rooted in brain capacities and in biological elements, intelligence can be improved and changed through practice and learning (e.g., Steinberg, 1985, 1989). Here exactly a question may come up; is governance in specific nations subject to "genes" of the society and to anchored/fixed rules that determine its evolvement with only minimal flexibility? Or the alternative is more likely, where all types of governance and governing agencies capable of learning and adoption, based on the floating/multiple principle of adaptation and greater flexibility? Let us keep this question in mind and return to it later when developing our models.

Undoubtedly, one of the major advocates of a more fluid, flexible and less-fixed approach was Gardner (1983). Gardner challenged the traditional view by arguing that human intelligence among people can improve their understanding, knowledge, skills, and talent about many aspects of life and with a variety of tools and methods. He returned to the original definitions of intelligence and reflected on the skills and abilities needed to solve problems within a culture. By so doing he opened a gate to a different look at intelligence. Based on current knowledge of the world, the brain, and the life in communities with learning orientations, Gardner tried to point to a variety of skill-sets which are desired by humans over a span of realms. He argued that intelligence could not be limited to one type of talent or a single group of skills, but instead could be classified into nine separate intelligence areas. He argued that humans possess all nine, but that everyone is strong in different intelligence areas and that most, if not all of them can be improved and changed. We will later extend on the relevancy of the idea of flexible and multiple intelligence to governance.

Gardner's original theory suggested seven types of intelligence among humans: (1) *Musical-rhythmic and harmonic;* sensitivity to sounds, rhythms, and music; (2) *Visual-spatial;* spatial judgment and the ability to visualize with the mind's eye; (3) *Linguistic-verbal:* facility and mastering of words and languages; (4) *Logical-mathematical:* logic skills, abstraction, reasoning, mastering numbers and critical thinking; (5) *Bodily-kinesthetic:* control of bodily motions and capacity to handle objects; (6) *Interpersonal:* sensitivity to others' moods, feelings, temperaments, motivations, and ability to cooperate within a group (7) *Intrapersonal:* introspective and self-reflective capacities, deep understanding of the self, its uniqueness, and dealing with emotions; In later years, he also mentioned additional forms of intelligence such as (8) *Naturalistic:* ability to recognize flora and fauna, to understand the natural world; and (9) *Existential;* spiritual capacities to deal with nonmaterialistic world for acquiring meaning and wellbeing of the self. More recently, and with the rise of the digital revolution, another type of *Digital Intelligence* was suggested which stands for a meta-intelligence composed of many other identified intelligences and stemmed from human interactions with digital computers and with other people using digital capacities (e.g., Adams, 2004).

3 Is There Multiple Intelligence in Governance?

The interest in intelligence has thus been shifted and extended from (1) fixed to floating models, (2) from single to multiple aspects, (3) from human to other-than-human entities, and (4) from individual to institutions, computers, and artificial intelligence. Nonetheless, all this rich knowledge, which was accumulated over nearly a century, have not diffused significantly into the realms of governance, political science, and public administration. Thus, we remain largely unclear about the meaning of intelligence for federal and state authorities, for local governance, for bureaucracies, for public and nonprofit organizations, for communities in their interaction with government, and for other policymaking agencies and institutions working with governance and around it.

Scholars agree today that individuals have the capacity of learning, understanding, and sense-making skills, such that can be relevant and spillover other entities as well. Such talents may have multiple aspects and reflections which are far beyond the individual level (Sternberg, 2020). Intelligence may be extended to groups, teams, social structures, institutions, and perhaps also machines and algorithms. Thus, can governance, as comprised by leading political and administrative individuals, teams, institutions and technologies be intelligent (or not) as well? And if they can, is this intelligence manifested in only one way or perhaps governments may be intelligent (or not) in various and multiple ways? Is this intelligence fixed or floating, and if it evolves and can be changed, what may be the mechanisms to alter it and maximize its potential?

To address at least some of these questions, we suggest gradual progress using an evolutionary model that will be explored in several stages. As a starting point we will specify a basic interdisciplinary model for understanding intelligence in the new "combat zone" of modern governance, open societies, advanced administrative, and political structures. This arena includes, beyond individuals, also higher collective levels of social players, abstractive levels of organizations and institutions, bureaucracies and political authorities, and the artificial medium of digital sphere where many actions and decisions of governments take place and apprehend. In such times citizens and governments interplay by dispatching and assimilating knowledge, information, and decisions using many new forms and methods that were not available nor acceptable only a few decades ago (e.g., social media, mobile apps, virtual reality, biometric tools, information mining, to name only few). We maintain that the current meaning of intelligence in governance cannot be fully understood unless new social constructs and digitization capacities are fully considered and integrated with other types of more traditional intelligence. Altogether these provide governance with comprehensive tools to deal with growing demand of public interests and with ambitious public policy challenges. Our core interdisciplinary model will allow us, at later stages, to explore more inclusive thinking through additional and advanced models of intelligence in governance.

4 Multiple Intelligence: An Interdisciplinary Perspective

Adopting Gardners' multiple intelligence theory in humans and adjusting it to the digital era directs us to focus on three main layers of intelligence: Human, Institutional, and Artificial. Accordingly, Figure 1 suggests a basic interdisciplinary model of multiple intelligence. The model provides an elementary set of relationships among these three layers of intelligence. A starting point would be a clear definition for each layer, which is followed by closer look into the scientific knowledge accumulated within each territory until today.

Human intelligence is regarded by psychologists as individuals' capacity to understand the reality around us, use skills and resources aimed at meeting goals, solving problems, and acquiring new knowledge. Consequently, when individuals operate in an institutional and organizational environment, they contribute their "talent" and "intelligence" to a bigger entity which combines these virtues and uses them in a collective manner. Such an aggregated level of intelligence forms *Institutions and organizations intelligence*. Quite distinctive from the first two types of intelligence, the digital era introduced us to

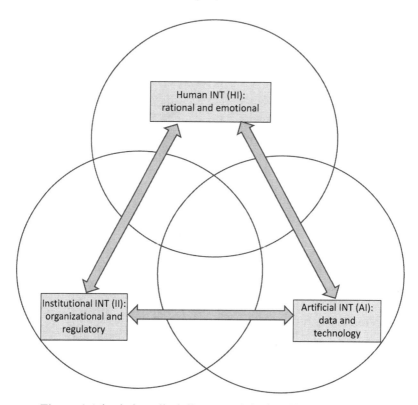

Figure 1 A basic interdisciplinary model of multiple intelligence

a nonhuman machinery type of *Artificial intelligence*. Such capacities involve humans as planners, architects, and developers of algorithms and machines with the goal of teaching them to learn and understand the environment much like humans. In the next sections we extend on the meaning of each type of intelligence and on how they relate with each other. This will allow us later to demonstrate their relevance and explanatory power to governments' actions and policies in the digital era.

4.1 Human Intelligence (HI): Rational and Emotional

Based on Gardner's theory of multiple intelligence, humans demonstrate many intellectual aspects that may be split between rational, conventional cognitive skills on one hand, and on the other hand non-rational, emotional cognitive skills. Most, if not all, of Gardner's core seven aspects of intelligence may be considered rational. Individuals may have cognitive skills and knowledge (i.e., intelligence) in musical-rhythmic and harmonic fields, in visual-spatial arenas, by linguistic-verbal talent, in logic and mathematics, in bodily-kinesthetic skills, in interpersonal relations, in intrapersonal abilities, in naturalistic awareness and skills, and in existential fields. All these pieces of talent and skills are based on rational thinking and/or knowledge that may be fixed as genetic/ natural or floating as learned and improved by training and practicing.

Yet in addition to all these types of rational intelligence, humans are also equipped with other types of intelligence that are less rational (e.g., Goleman, 2006). One of them is emotional intelligence which is entirely different from the other rational types. The construct of Emotional Intelligence (EI) was first coined by Salovey and Mayer (1990) who defined it as "the ability to perceive accurately, appraise, and express emotion; the ability to access and/or generate feelings when they facilitate thought; the ability to understand emotion and emotional knowledge; and the ability to regulate emotions to promote emotional and intellectual growth" (p. 10). Salovey and Mayer's (1990) model assumes that EI comprises of the interrelated skills of self-awareness, managing emotions, motivating oneself, empathy, and handling relationships. Using quite a similar definition, Wong and Law (2002) and Law et al., (2004) developed an ability-based four branch model in which EI is subdivided into four components: (1) Self Emotional Appraisal (SEA) – the ability to understand one's deep emotions and be able to express these emotions naturally; (2) Others' Emotional Appraisal (OEA) – the ability to perceive and understand the emotions of those people around us; (2) Regulation Of Emotions (ROE) – the ability to regulate and control one's own emotions; and (4) Use of Emotions (UOE) – the ability of individuals to make use of one's emotions by directing them toward constructive activities and personal performance. Hence, both rational and emotional intelligence constitute the intellectual individual anchors for an upper level of intelligence, the one at the collective institutional level.

4.2 Institutional Intelligence (II): Organizational and Regulatory

Institutional intelligence, frequently also named organizational intelligence, represents the capability of an institution/organization to comprehend and create knowledge relevant to their goals and markets. It is the intellectual capacity of the entire organization, built up on its members and overall resources capacities. Therefore, some studies find similarities between this type of intelligence and collective intelligence (e.g., Woolley et al., 2010) which stands for the distributed knowledge or capability in human systems in which the whole is greater than the sum of the parts (e.g., Kittur et al., 2009; Woolley, 2011). In fact, institutional intelligence is comprised of both organizational and regulatory components. The organizational facet refers to any type of company, firm, or agency, whereas regulatory intelligence is more relevant to public sector organizations who hold wider responsibilities toward citizens. Overall, studies suggest that institutional intelligence, both organizational and regulatory, creates great potential value for companies and firms to figure out where their strengths and weaknesses lie in responding to change and complexity. As much as governance is concerned, the potential value of institutional intelligence is by increasing public interest and public goods with better knowledge, skills, policy decisions, and public performance that work for citizens in general, not just for customers in limited markets.

The idea of aggregated intelligence at the institutional and organizational level goes as far as Wilensky's (1967) pioneering work on *Organizational Intelligence: Knowledge and Policy in Government and Industry.* More than three decades prior to the digital revolution of the 1990s, Wilensky suggested that strengthening pluralistic societies must involve the flow of intelligence, mostly in the form of information relevant to policy. However, such increasing amounts of information that are assumed to lead to greater intelligence are both a source of power and a source of confusion and ignorance due to their overload on organizations, on individuals in and around them, and on governance and the markets. Since the publication of the book more than half a century ago, the amount of information in institutions has grown exponentially. But has their intelligence grown as well? The digital revolution helped institutions (governmental and nongovernmental) to acquire information, store and restore it in big-date forms, and use it more effectively. Institutions accumulate and maintain big-data sources and expect individuals, both inside and outside those institutions, to use them wisely in making decisions and determining policies. But the crossroads of integrating individual intelligence with institutional intelligence is far from trivial (e.g., in HR decisions, in making strategic market or policy choices, in handling customers and citizens etc.) and becomes more difficult as the digital gap between individuals and machines broadens. Humans are not capable mentally and emotionally of digesting such big amounts of information. They must be supported by machines that help them understand, interpret, process, and use the data. Machines, on the other hand, depend on humans to feed them with effective algorithms, preferences, selections, and criteria, such that help in making proper use of the data. At the Institutional level, many organizations are on continuous chase for closing this gap. But as long as the gap remains significant, overall institutional intelligence remains behind human intelligence and thus also far from optimal.

Hence, studies in later years developed the idea of institutional intelligence further with the hope that the gap can be minimized significantly. Glynn (1996) develops the concept of organizational intelligence as quite similar to innovation and overall individual intelligence (i.e., as purposeful information processing that enables adaptation to environmental demands). Organizational intelligence, however, is conceptualized as a social outcome and is related to individual intelligence by mechanisms of aggregation, cross-level transference, and distribution of knowledge. He suggests a conceptual framework that relates types and levels of intelligence, moderated by contextual factors, to the two stages of the organizational innovation process: initiation and implementation. McMaster (1996: 3) and March (1999) build on the institutional theory to see organizational intelligence as a capacity of the entire corporation to "gather information, to innovate, to generate knowledge, and to act effectively based on the knowledge it has generated." This can be done with internal HR resources or by emulation of other intelligent institutions. Thus, they suggest that institutional intelligence is getting more and more critical in the digital age, especially with the rise of artificial intelligence (AI).

4.3 Artificial Intelligence (AI): Data and Technology

Artificial intelligence is the talent we relate to computers, algorithms, and other machines in our environment. AI is a new generation of technologies "capable of interacting with the environment and aiming to simulate human intelligence" (Glikson & Woolley, 2020: 627). These types of modern digital tools use data (and increasingly bigdata) created and developed by humans in a dual track method of both processing and producing such data. Yet rich discussion continues about the option that such machines will develop autonomous intelligence independent of the humans that originally created them. This discussion is, however, at the abstractive philosophical level. Theoretically and practically, we see AI as referring to machines mimicking human behavior in terms of cognitive functions.

In recent years, artificial intelligence has had a tremendous impact on every field of our life, and on many aspects of governance (Wiltz et al., 2019). Numerous definitions exist for AI and its different types. They all point to exceptional capabilities of this technology to help humans understand problems faster, better, and with greater power. Whereas most studies on AI come from an applied technological, engineering, or computerized perspectives, others focus on specific relevancy of AI to subfield of applied sciences such as medicine and health, psychology, education, management, neuroscience, or environment (to name only few). In most studies, AI strongly relates with new techniques to handle big data sources that allow machines and algorithms to develop far-reaching processing power, tracking, analyzing and especially decision-making skills with no human hand involved during the process.

Intelligent systems become dominant in our lives. They include variants of infrastructures, tools and methods of Information technology (IT), Machine Learning (ML), Deep Learning (DL), Big Data (BD), Open Data (OD), Cyber/ Cyberspace and social media, Mobile Technologies (MT), Internet and

Metaverse, Bots, Robots, and other algorithms. Saghiri et al. (2022) suggest that as the usage of such intelligent tools and systems increases, the number of new challenges increases. Among the most significant challenges that are relevant for governance today are security, privacy, safety, fairness, robustness, and energy consumption, which have been reported during the development of intelligent systems. Obviously, AI depends on human intelligence and closely relates with institutional intelligence. It builds on humans' capacity to form such machines and feed them with orders and data, and it feeds back our human and institutional intelligence with new implications and extensive understanding resulting from this powerful processing capacity of the new technologies. Thus, the recent development of human-level intelligence cannot be fully materialized without reliable AI systems.

When taken together, human intelligence, institutional intelligence, and artificial intelligence are the core concepts on which an interdisciplinary model of multiple intelligence in governance should be designed. As we tried to demonstrate so far, these three types of intelligence are closely related, feeding one other with knowledge, data, and understanding of our complex public environment. Thus, we postulate our first proposition:

P1: *A basic interdisciplinary model of multiple intelligence comprises human (rational & emotional), institutional (organizational & regulatory), and artificial (data & technology) intelligences.*

5 Toward Intelligent Governance: An Evolutionary Model

The basic interdisciplinary model of multiple intelligence as suggested above is our starting point of the next steps toward other evolutionary models for intelligent governance. The three-phase evolution will be presented and rationalized in three separate main blocks. First, we will introduce an *interdisciplinary model of multiple intelligence in governance* and explain it in detail. Next, we will enrich this model with additional mediating constructs to create a *coupled interdisciplinary model of intelligence in governance*. Based on the coupled interdisciplinary model, we will explore a third and final evolutionary block of *comprehensive model for intelligence in governance*. For each model we will also present propositions that more explicitly foster explanatory relationships which may inspire future studies.

5.1 An interdisciplinary Model of Multiple Intelligence in Governance

Figure 2 suggests that the basic interdisciplinary model of multiple intelligence is highly applicable and relevant for governance and public administration.

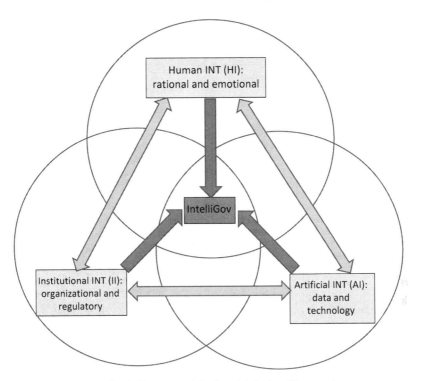

Figure 2 An interdisciplinary model of multiple intelligence in governance

We define intelligent governance as *a combination of human intelligence (HI), institutional intelligence (II), and artificial intelligence (AI) for better use of information, data, and knowledge to improve the effectiveness and efficiency of government decision-making, policies, and public management.* This combination is not trivial as it brings together different levels of analysis. We acknowledge the obstacles in the social sciences to integrating pieces of knowledge from multilevel sources. To do so we must rely on the most basic level of human intelligence and ensure that it can be elevated to deal with higher levels of institutional and artificial machine intelligence. We maintain that intelligence in governance is composed of the previous generic human, institutional, and artificial elements that not only speak to each other but also directly affect a variety of governing and administrative entities, agencies, and individuals, and do so in many ways. The goal of intelligent governance is to advance the ability of government bodies to solve problems, make informed reliable decisions, and provide quality services to citizens by evidence-based management of limited public resources. But what exactly does each of the three elements mean? One approach to answering this question is exploring how one level can build on the other levels. The next sections elaborate on these questions in two parts. First, we carefully look at each layer of intelligence (HI, II, AI) in the context of governance. Then, we try to explain the meaning of each layer in the context of the other layers and determine their relevance for the public sphere of governance and public administration.

5.1.1 Human Intelligence (HI) in Governance

Human intelligence in governance is comprised of both the rational and the emotional aspects of involving people in public policy and public administration activities. The rational part of human intelligence in governance is based on the abilities of civil servants, and of other stakeholders at the economic, political, and social spheres to understand problems of public interest, process them and consider proper solutions to meet public needs and public goals. This dimension of rationality in intelligent governance strongly relates with several components of Gardners' multiple types of intelligence. For example, they relate with *Visual-spatial intelligence* as public servants need, at times, to have spatial judgment of the environment, and the ability to visualize specific situations and cases with the mind's eye (e.g., in urban planning, in environmental considerations, in street-level bureaucracy functions). They also relate with *Linguistic-verbal intelligence* which deals with the facility and mastering of words and languages in dealing with written materials on policies and decisions, in delivering written and oral messages both within public organizations, and to external audience such as citizens and other collaborators in public initiatives. Finally, the rational part of human intelligence in governance involves *Logical-mathematical capacities* that use logic skills, abstraction, reasoning, criticism, and mastering numbers when evaluating the social, economic, and political costs of public policies and decisions, finance, budgets, and rational for evidence-based policymaking. Such abilities are important in many situations asking policymakers and line public managers to deal with procedures and processes in a logical sequence which may be influential in various public fields, from public healthcare to education, national defence and homeland security, and all other aspects of tactic and strategic decisions making at the federal, national, and local governance levels.

Another aspect of Gardner's multiple theory of intelligence is the emotional and interpersonal ability that focuses on sensitivity to others' moods, emotions and feelings, temperaments, motivations, and ability to cooperate within a group. The emotional part of human intelligence in governance has been discussed from at least two perspectives that, despite some differences, have many similarities. The first perspective builds on studies such as Berman and West (2008) and Vigoda-Gadot and Meisler (2010) who looked at Emotional

Intelligence (EI) of civil servants as highly relevant in public administration. The second perspective used Emotional Labor (EL) as another concept which is important for better management of public organizations and public personnel (Guy, Newman, & Mastracci, 2008). EI is a considered distinct construct from EL. The former may be thought of as the ability to perceive, understand, appraise, and express emotion, coupled with the ability to generate and regulate feelings (Salovey & Mayer, 1990; Mayer & Salovey, 1997; Ciarrochi, Forgas, & Mayer, 2001). The latter refers to "the exercise of emotional skills to get the job done" (Guy & Lee, 2015: 261). Therefore, the abilities allowing individuals to perform EL successfully are those grounded in EI (e.g., Hsieh, 2009; Joseph & Newman, 2010). Both EI and EL play a major role in internal and external relationships of government personnel with a variety of stakeholders. They were found to be positively related to various work-related constructs, such as: job satisfaction (e.g. Vigoda-Gadot & Meisler, 2010; Brunetto et al., 2012), affective commitment (e.g. Levitats & Vigoda-Gadot, 2017), leadership effectiveness (Kotzé & Venter, 2011), well-being (Brunetto et al., 2012), public service motivation and service quality (Levitats & Vigoda-Gadot, 2017), and employees engagement (Levitats & Vigoda-Gadot, 2020). It may thus be argued that EI and EL help foster a more intelligent public sector environment. They create a positive atmosphere that helps people make better use of the information and knowledge around them to improve the quality of their work and their work outcomes.

5.1.2 Institutional Intelligence (II) in Governance

Despite several significant contributions to the study of organizational intelligence (e.g., Wilensky, 1967; Glynn, 1996; Smith, 2017) studies in governance, political science and public administration quite overlooked the potential of inquiring into governances' organizational or institutional intelligence. Although institutional intelligence and organizational intelligence quite overlap, we favor using the former concept as it better relates with the spirit of governance as bureaucratic in nature, reflecting the actions of complex public administration agencies and the public sphere in general. Thus, Institutional intelligence in governance may be regarded as an extension of the organizational intelligence concept into the realm of bureaucracies, public agencies, and governing institutions, with a focus on their unique normative standing as seeking public interests and public goods in modern societies. It is based on a major theoretical stream of institutionalism in politics, new institutionalism, and new governance (e.g., March & Olsen, 1984; Ostrom, 1990; Carrigan & Coglianese, 2011). Based on the major role of administrative and political institutions in society, institutional intelligence may be defined as *the broad information and knowledge processing in governmental and semi-governmental bureaucracies or agencies that produces better learning and coping mechanisms to deal with public goals.* It includes organizational-level understanding of the public interest, the institutional planned and implemented policy aimed at advancing public goods, and the promotions of public values by regulatory mechanisms of the institution for better serving citizens and other stakeholders.

Institutional intelligence in governance may thus be seen as built on the generic concept of organizational intelligence, which is largely a collective type of intelligence in the workplace (e.g., Woolley, 2011). However, whereas the organizational factor of institutional intelligence is generic to all institutions, administrative and governing organizations also hold another form of intelligence that builds on their important regulatory responsibility. The formal regulatory factor is under the sole auspice of governmental agencies. This is due to their responsibility to maintain, safeguard, and advance public interests wherever conventional open markets fail to do so. In such cases, governing bodies are there to make sure that data, information, and knowledge are used intelligently for constructive public interests only. Regulation in food and drugs, healthcare, communication, energy, welfare, and environments protection are only few territories where governance institutional intelligence dominate and has no similarity with any other market. To do so, governing institutions are expected to demonstrate their regulatory wisdom, and maintain institutional intelligence alongside values such as transparency, accountability, responsiveness, and overall responsibility to citizens. These standards are only secondary within private and for-profit organizations. Nevertheless, studies on governance' institutional intelligence are scarce. Studies usually refer to "good governance," "smart governance," "sound governance," or "wise governance" (e.g., Meijer & Bolivar, 2016; Grossi et al., 2020) at the federal, national, or local levels (e.g., smart cities; Preira et al., 2018) with a goal of explaining what makes one governmental agency smarter, wiser, and generally better performing than others. Yet most of the discussion in this filed is oriented toward technological developments, data-based infrastructures, or cyber and communication inspirations that explore the capacity of public organizations to govern data or to apply AI governance tools (e.g., Janssen et al., 2020; Radu, 2021).

Virtanen and Vakkuri (2016) suggest that the intelligence of public organizations is a distributed knowledge system or sense-making community (Choo, 1998; Tsoukas, 2005). This theoretical view focuses on knowledge resources a public-sector organization deploys which are created in the process of making sense of the knowledge. Thus, the intelligence of a public organization comprises both knowledge-based decision-making and customer-centered thinking based on the service mission of governance. Inspired by the idea of collective intelligence in organizations, institutional public intelligence draws substance both from within public agencies (the collective intelligence of public servants) and from outside the public system (the collective intelligence of stakeholders such as citizens, private-sector, and third-sector collaborators). To get closer to these goals, institutional intelligence in governance relies on intelligent structures that allow a smooth flow of information, intelligent leadership, intelligent procedures, and reliable regulations that protect public interest, public safety, and public welfare. Intelligent platforms are needed to support flexible and adaptive policymaking. This can be done by following performance management standards and applying sophisticated information management tools. In addition, institutional intelligence in governance comprises citizens-sensitive innovative culture and political wisdom, as well as a spirit of transparency and accountability to citizens. These factors exist only marginally or not at all in private-sector organizations.

We thus expect institutional intelligence in governance to use knowledge-management systems based on triple elements: humans, organizations, and machines. They should also be comprehensive in the way they take a policy issue and process it from the initial stage of generating ideas to final stages of implementation and assessment of results. Hence, institutional-level intelligence in governance strongly relates with the field on performance management in the public sector. It allows analyses of more and less intelligent policies, decisions, knowledge processing, implementation, regeneration of explanations, and promotion of solutions to new public policy and public management problems. Institutional intelligence in governance builds on intelligent public organizations which are expected to (1) understand performance-management systems' logic in terms of how information metrics are linked with target-setting in the strategy process, and (2) develop retrospective and prospective types of performance indicators which can be deployed in performance metrics and make sure that outcome indicators at the institutional level really measure the impact of a specific public organization on the society. Consequently, studies also mention resilience as key feature of intelligent public policymaking, program implementation and business intelligence of public organizations (e.g., McManus et al. 2008). Resilience is related with institutionally intelligent governance, especially during emergency times or global crises when bureaucracies and public administration play central role in safeguarding the public interest (e.g., Vigoda-Gadot et al, 2023b).

5.1.3 Artificial Intelligence (AI) in Governance

Over the last decade, studies on AI in governance are on the rise mainly because of global progress in technology and growing expectations for better governance performance. AI becomes dominant in almost every field of governance;

however, our knowledge in this field remains rather limited. Recently, Wirtz, Langer, and Fenner (2019) used quantitative and qualitative analysis of 189 selected articles to show that the current state of research on AI in governance is heterogeneous and thematically and methodologically unbalanced. Many studies on AI in the governance context focus on politics and administration, while more specific application areas receive less attention. Studies to date focus in detail on changes to existing government structures, while the creation of entirely new structures due to new AI technologies is given less consideration.

Henman (2020) suggests that AI arising from the use of machine learning is rapidly being developed and deployed by governments across the globe to enhance operations, public services, and compliance and security activities. He mentions four public administration challenges to deploying AI in public administration: (1) accuracy, bias, and discrimination; (2) legality, due process and administrative justice; (3) responsibility, accountability, transparency and explainability; and (4) power, compliance and control. Another study by Taeihagh (2021) also suggests that governments are expected to manage and regulate these socio-technical transitions. Integration of AI in governance may increase economic efficiency and improve quality of services for better life of citizens, but this positive impact does not come without a price. Using AI in governance poses risks, both to bureaucracies in the form of political and administrative institutions that may become overdependent in AI, and to stakeholders such as citizens and collaborators with governance who may lose the human touch with governance. Major risks for the public interest are the misuse of open and big data sources by unauthorized parties, the risk to privacy and financial stability at the individual and national levels, and threats like cyberattacks by machines on government institutions that may foster conflicts, instability, and crises within and between nations. Today, AI is largely being used in the public sector for automated decision-making, for chatbots to provide information and advice, and for public safety and security. It is implemented across almost all levels of government functions and especially in public healthcare (e.g., Panch et al., 2019), in public transportation (e.g., Kumar et al., 2021), in national and homeland security (e.g., Park & Jones-Jang, 2022), in public education (e.g., Cukurova et al., 2020), and further attracts more comparative global view (e.g., de Sousa et al., 2019).

Empirical efforts to examine AI in governance provide interesting findings. Young, Bullock, and Lecy (2019) suggest that public administration research has documented a shift in the locus of discretion away from street-level bureaucrats to systems-level bureaucracies. This was a result of new information communication technologies that automate bureaucratic processes, and thus shape access to resources and decisions around enforcement and punishment.

They introduce the concept of artificial discretion as a theoretical framework to help public managers consider the impact of AI as they face decisions about whether and how to implement it. Artificial discretion is operationalized by criteria of effectiveness, efficiency, equity, manageability, and political feasibility, and findings suggest three principal ways by which it can improve administrative discretion at the task level: (1) increasing scalability, (2) decreasing cost, and (3) improving quality. However, artificial discretion raises serious concerns with respect to equity, manageability, and political desirability and feasibility. De Sousa et al. (2019) conducted a literature review on AI in the public sector and show that public service, economic affairs, and environmental protection are the functions of government with the most studies related to AI. They suggest that policies and ethical implications of the use of AI permeate all layers of application of this technology and the solutions can generate value for functions of government. Quite in the same vein, Wang, Xie, and Li (2024) use Simon's decision-making theory to compare the effects of AI versus humans on discretion, client meaningfulness, and willingness-to-implement. They examine the moderating role of different types of decisions and find that AI usage has a negative effect on perceived discretion and a positive effect on willingness-to-implement. Conversely, they conclude that non-programmed decisions tend to have a positive effect on both perceived discretion and willingness-to-implement.

Some studies are more positive about the impact of AI on governments outcomes. They argue that public institutions should take advantage of the technological revolution not only to renew their technical capacity, but especially to handle conceptual and organizational problems (e.g., Mikalef et al., 2022). Artificial intelligence and robotics can be the drivers of radical institutional and organizational reforms and strategic changes in public and governmental institutions. Beyond speeding up processes and improving efficiency AI may create a paradigmatic revolution in different models and cultures of the administration (bureaucratic, managerial, regulatory, and governance) to achieve greater institutional strength. AI and intelligent robotics may foster a solid bureaucratic model that is objective, neutral, fast, and efficient, and at the same time avoiding negative impacts such as excessive rigidity and corporate drifts (bureaucracy without bureaucrats). As a result, new models of public administrations will become more intelligent and democratic, collaborative, creative, and innovative but also solid, predictable, and constant. Hence, the success of governance and administration of the future largely depends on its institutional wisdom and intelligence capabilities, as supported by vast AI infrastructures

Recently, O'Shaughnessy et al. (2022) used SEM technique to examine underlying factors and mechanisms that drive attitudes toward the use and governance of AI across six policy-relevant applications. They used surveys of both US adults (N = 3,524) and technology workers enrolled in an online computer science master's degree program ($N = 425$). Findings revealed that the cultural values of individualism, egalitarianism, general risk aversion, and techno-skepticism are important drivers of AI attitudes toward government and that experts are more supportive of AI use in governance but not its regulation. Bullock (2019) found a relationship between AI, discretion, and bureaucracy. It was argued that AI, as an advanced information communication technology tool (ICT), changes both the nature of human discretion within a bureaucracy and the structure of bureaucracies. The complexity and uncertainty they fuse into administrative systems redefines tasks and responsibilities and thus discretion and decision-making are strongly influenced by such intelligence. Therefore, the improvements in AI can help improve the overall quality of administration.

In view of the above accumulated knowledge, we suggest that better understanding intelligence in and around governance calls for an integrative look into the essence of this concept, one that interrelates HI, II, and AI in governance. Thus, overall intelligence in governance is affected by human, institutional, and artificial factors that are positively related with each other and altogether make an integrative impact on governing bodies. The main challenge in this context is combining knowledge about intelligent governance from different levels of analysis. Human intelligence is at the root of science and knowledge. Without it, none of the other levels of intelligence would have emerged. People accumulate knowledge, create institutions, and produce machines. They allow all other types of intelligence to develop and grow. Therefore, we build on the individual level of analysis as the critical source of intelligent governance. Thus, our second proposition is an extension of the first proposition into the realm of governance and suggests that:

P2: Intelligent Governance is positively affected by human (rational & emotional), institutional (organizational & regulatory), and artificial (data & technology) intelligences.

5.2 A Coupled Interdisciplinary Model of Multiple Intelligence in Governance

Figure 3 takes our evolutionary model one step forward by focusing on the coupling role of three new elements: Social Intelligence (SI), Human–Machine Interaction Intelligence (HMII), and Business Intelligence (BI). We will argue that these mid-range types of intelligence are important mediators between core intelligent elements of HI, II, and AI, and that they help in better understanding

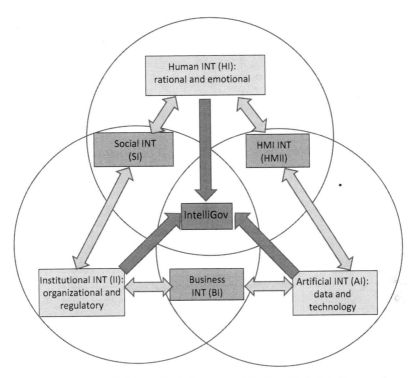

Figure 3 A coupled interdisciplinary model of multiple intelligence in governance

how overall intelligent governance is structured and how it evolves. First, we start by briefly reviewing the meaning and scholarly knowledge about each one of these elements. Next, we will explain how each one serves as mediators in the evolving model.

5.2.1 Social Intelligence (SI) in Governance

Social and interpersonal intelligence was part of Gardenr's original model of multiple intelligence. However, it was mentioned many years earlier by Hunt (1928) as a major component of human skills. According to Hunt's study social intelligence is the capacity to deal with people and social relationships. Later studies suggested strong anchors to this idea in the theory of mind which reflects the capacity of humans to understand others using mental models and interpretation of beliefs, desires, intentions, emotions, thoughts, and behaviors (e.g., Baron-Cohen, 1991). These are evident in people but also in other species (e.g., Apperly & Butterfill, 2009). It can be assessed by various social abilities such as observing human behavior, understanding social situations, and the general talent to constructively get along with other individuals within formal or informal groups. Such social skills are based on various capacities to understand facial expressions, recognition of the mental state of the speaker, memory for names and faces, and sense of humor. Thus, social intelligence represents the capacity to know oneself, to know others, and to effectively manage relationships with others. Therefore, studies also suggest understanding its meaning through the concept of collective intelligence in humans (e.g., Bloom, 2000; Kittur et al., 2009; Woolley et al., 2011). All these ideas are univocal about social intelligence being a learned skill which is gradually developed over time, from experience with social interactions with others. It is a learned ability to understand self-actions and the responses of others to one's actions. As such, it is significantly related with the emotional aspects of intelligence in governance such as EI and EL. Goleman (2006) further used social neuroscience research to propose that social intelligence is made up of social awareness (including empathy, attunement, empathic accuracy, and social cognition) and social facility (including synchrony, self-presentation, influence, and concern). Hence, it implies that our social relationships have a direct effect on our mental and physical health, as well as on our burnout and resilience. The deeper the relationship the deeper the impact. Effects include blood flow, breathing, mood such as fatigue and depression, mental stress and distress, and weakening of the immune system.

It is not hard to see how all these symptoms are relevant to the arena of citizens-governance relations in many cases of interactions with public authorities, both physically and digitally. Thus, social (or interpersonal/collective) intelligence in and around governance institutions constitutes unique meaning. The social environment of governance and the individuals working for governance and around it is complex. Many stakeholders interact with each other and with government officials to create value for the public. During these interactions, citizens frequently experience frustration rooted in dealing with long and tedious bureaucratic procedures. Public servants, and especially street-level bureaucrats, experience burnout resulting from intensive interactions with highly demanding citizens. Within the new public management spirit, these social interactions of street-level bureaucrats with citizens-as-customers result in stress and tension for all the involved parties. Thus, social intelligence, infused by both rational and emotional human facets, becomes essential in better dealing with such conflictual relationships (e.g., Eshuis, de Boer, & Klijn, 2023).

Moreover, the interactions among these individuals and between them and formal authorities requires skills and talents that are beyond conventional capacities in daily social interactions. For example, SI in governance involves the effective use of influential political skills, the implementation of negotiation abilities, and the need to build coalitions to support one's opinion or ideas (e.g., Vigoda-Gadot, 2007). These are essential in any organization but are extremely important when policy is formatted and developed at the national and local level. Jean Piaget suggested that intelligence is not a fixed attribute, but a complex hierarchy of information-processing skills underlying an adaptive equilibrium between the individual and the environment (Piaget, 1972). As the environment of public organizations and governance is highly complex and requires specific political talents, social/interpersonal/collective intelligence becomes an essential mediator between the individual and the bureaucratic institution. Since low socially intelligent individuals may not have skills necessary to communicate with citizens and/or co-workers, they may be more successful with public jobs of minimal interactions with others. On the other hand, socially intelligent individuals may be an asset for governance, especially as street-level bureaucrats (to reduce tension with citizens) or as policymakers (to effectively lead groups into their missions). They may be highly productive in jobs that involve direct contact and communication with citizens and other stakeholders (Lavee et al., 2018). They may work exceptionally well and exhibit high public service motivation (Rauhaus, 2022) when working with others, and positively affecting them. Finally, as SI skills may decline in the digital age due to lower levels of conventional social interactions, governance may be affected as well. Since SI is a learned practice, it is a major concern for public organizations who manage relations with the public. Thus, governance should care about minimizing deficiencies in SI among both service providers and policymakers on one hand, and on the other hand among service recipients and interactors with governmental authorities.

5.2.2 HMI Intelligence (HMII) in Governance

Interactions between human intelligence and machine intelligence is a fast-growing field of study named HMI (Human–Machine Interactions). Understanding and developing new devices and architectures relating machines capacities with humans needs, expectations, and skills is almost a discipline of its own, rooted in the crossroad of engineering, natural, and exact sciences on one hand, and on the other hand social and behavioral sciences (e.g., Singh & Kumar, 2021). With the rapid penetration of technology to governance at all types of services, jobs, and policy levels such an interaction may become a crucial factor affecting citizens' satisfaction, trust in governance, the effectiveness and efficiency of policies, and many other public values, outputs, and outcomes.

When speaking about intelligent HMI, studies break new ground to another type of intelligence, one that builds capacities not independently for the machine or the human, but rather for the systems and interfaces that relates them. Studies suggested that the idea of intelligent interfaces appeared at the beginning of the 1980s and was defined as those systems that provides tools to help minimize the cognitive distance between the mental model that the user has of the task and the way in which the task is presented to the user by the computer when the task is performed (Hancock & Clugnell, 1989; Kolski & Strugeon, 1998). Studies on HMI intelligence have expanded since then. More recently, these capacities have evolved and are described as Intelligent User Interfaces (IUIs). They generate HMIs that seek to improve the efficiency, effectiveness, and naturalness of human–machine interaction by representing, reasoning, and acting on models of the user, domain, task, discourse, and media (Concalves et al., 2019). They use AI, Human–Computer Interaction (HCI), Software Engineering (SE), and other techniques to promote more natural and usable HMI. Such interfaces are strongly anchored in software systems, capable to intelligently adapt themselves to their users (Sanchez et al., 2017). For this, the behavioral characteristics of the users are stored in different models such as user model, device or platform model, environment model, interaction model, task model, and others (Concalves et al., 2019). Thus, IUIs change their behavior according to the models to adapt to a person or task or, more generally to the context (Ross, 2000).

The relevance of IUI to governance is clear. As we demonstrated earlier, governing organizations and public agencies rapidly adopt digital tools and methods in all areas of public service. One example is the use of intelligent tutorial systems in education (e.g., Schuller, 2015), but also in policymaking, in street-level bureaucrats' activity, and in other territories of public interest. Intelligent User Interface in governance is well demonstrated by the need to be flexible with service receivers and adopt to social norms and human behavior that are going through rapid change vis-à-vis the digital transformation in governance. Examples for the potential impact of IUI in governance are many. How people respond to the use of cameras in public spheres depends on time, context and the people themselves. Citizens dealing with bots, robots, and algorithms instead of face-to-face interactions with public servants may respond differently based on the situation, type of interaction, mood, and environment. Other questions emerge as well: What is the impact of such IUIs on citizens' trust in governance and on civil servants' approach and treatment of citizens? Can we develop flexible enough IUI systems to deal with changing audiences, situations, and contexts in public spheres like social services, education, public health, public safety, environmental contexts, etc.? How potential answers to these questions differ across ethnically diverse people, nations and cultures? And what about our specific trust in these intelligent technologies and interfaces? This later question was recently discussed by

Glikson and Woolley (2020) who suggested that the form of AI and interface representation (robot, virtual, and embedded) and its level of machine intelligence (i.e., its capabilities) is an important antecedent to the development of users' cognitive and emotional trust. Nevertheless, we currently remain quite in the dark when trying to answer most of the above questions and concerns. A major step forward, however, is the consideration of HMII and IUIs as part of the bigger puzzle of intelligence in governance.

5.2.3 Business Intelligence (BI) in Governance

Alongside the previously discussed mediating components of intelligence (i.e., SI and HMII) there is an additional facet that deserves our attention. This is Business Intelligence (BI) which appears to mediate between Institutional Intelligence (II) and Artificial Intelligence (AI). The term business intelligence represents knowledge and understanding of the interconnections between bureaucracies and machines in any organization, and even more profoundly in the public sphere. Thus, at times, BI is considered similar with organizational intelligence. However, BI is in fact a very specific type of intelligence that combines organizational and digital capacities at the institutional level. BI is usually defined as strategies and technologies used by enterprises for the data analysis and management of business information. It is a managerial philosophy and a tool used to help organizations manage and refine business information with the objective of making better decisions (Gilad & Gilad, 1986). More recently Smith (2017) suggested that despite some bad connotation we frequently relate to social and organizational institutions (e.g., as typically overloaded with red-tape and lacking enough sensitivity to individuals), they all carry vital business and managerial intelligence that may benefit us. He defines such intelligence roughly as the wisdom of working effectively within an organization. Today, such wisdom heavily relies on technology and information systems. In every institution, leaders, directors, executives, board members, key stakeholders, and employees interact in many ways. Such interactions involve more and more technology and computerized data. The more constructive this interaction is for the greatest benefit of all involved, the greater the business intelligence of the entire institution.

Thus, BI is strongly affiliated with the new digital revolution and with computerized data-based tools, and the capacity to use them for business and management goals. Examples for BI are many and vary across organizational functions such as finance, marketing and sales, customer/citizens' services, HRM, and operation. They build on four main pillars: (1) big data from a variety of sources that are centralized and accessible; (2) business analytics and data management tools and expertise to analyze the data and produce desirable outcomes; (3) business and management tools to monitor and analyze progress toward specific goals; (4) a wise user interface for quick access and use. Thus, problems such as targeting specific populations and markets, finding sources for technical or other professional support among other stakeholders, and analyzing environmental hazards are typical for business intelligence use. Recently, Talaoui & Kohtamaki (2021) review 120 influential articles over a course of 35 years to provide an integrative view of this type of intelligence. They found eight dimensions of antecedents that contribute to BI: environmental; organizational; managerial; individual; BI process; strategic outcomes; firm performance outcomes; decision-making; and organizational intelligence.

Business Intelligence and its eight dimensions of antecedents are highly relevant for governance. They involve managerial and administration values, and a business-technology spirit that allows problem-solving orientation of public service employees. Business Intelligence is useful for public management techniques and the use of data and information in managing people and improving services for citizens. This data is growing rapidly into Big-Data, and similarly BI in governance becomes more and more important. Furthermore, it well integrates into the NPM and post-NPM doctrines by implementing new data sources to acquire greater performance, more understanding of citizens expectations, and improvement of responsiveness, accountability and transparency of information and knowledge in a business-like governance. It is different from II on one hand and, on the other hand from AI as it combines the knowledge gained in both to allow constructive operation of bureaucrats at all levels (policymakers, middle management staff, and street-level bureaucrats). Studies on BI in a global context also identify the impact of cultural diversity and values which may be highly influential in the governance context (e.g., Munoz, 2018). In such an environment BI brings together knowledge accumulated at the institutional level of policymakers, mission groups and thinktanks of specific cultures, with the knowledge and data provided by machines and algorithms in those cultures, for the agile and effective running of bureaucratic systems.

Based on the review, rational, and synthesis suggested so far, we postulate the third proposition in three subset parts.

P3a: Social Intelligence (SI) mediate the relationship between Human Intelligence (HI) and Institutional Intelligence (II) in governance.

P3b: HMI Intelligence (HMII) mediates the relationship between Human Intelligence (HI) and Artificial Intelligence (AI) in governance.

P3 c: Business Intelligence (BI) mediates the relationship between Institutional Intelligence (II) and Artificial Intelligence (AI) in governance.

6 IntelliGov: A Comprehensive Interdisciplinary Model of Governance Intelligence

Figure 4 presents a final stage of our evolutionary modeling. It explores the *IntelliGov* model, which is a comprehensive interdisciplinary framework for multiple intelligent in governance. IntelliGov builds on the previous mid-range models and the conceptual arsenal on variants of intelligence from diverse disciplines. Following Gardner's (1983) multiple intelligence framework and adjusting it to governance we define IntelliGov as the *integration of HI, II, AI, SI, HMII, & BI for better public management and policy in and around governing institutions.* This final stage of model construction adds another loop to the previous models suggesting significant reciprocal interrelationships between HMII, SI, and BI, and a direct effect of each one of them on IntelliGov. To explore these interrelationships further we try to rationalize on each one of them separately. Let us examine the HMII ⟷ BI, HMII ⟷ SI, SI ⟷ BI relationships.

First, we expect that HMII will be positively related with BI. The rational is based on the idea that HMII may contribute to the institutional business

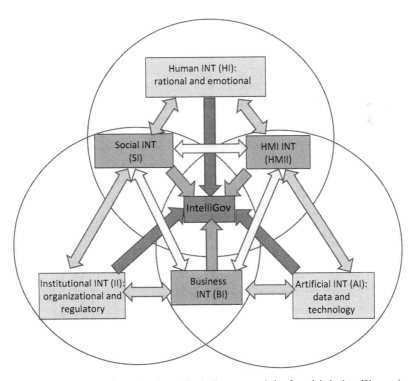

Figure 4 A comprehensive interdisciplinary model of multiple intelligent in governance (the IntelliGov Model)

capacities of learning, better management, and better decisions at the institutional level, by using IUI and intelligent technological interfaces as a source of tutoring, data and information that works well with humans (e.g., Schuller, 2015). Improving the interface with humans is at the heart of IUI and HMII, and governance is seeking such better interface as well. Thus, HMII and BI are mutually inspired. The use of HMII for strengthening BI can be done in many ways. One example is improving decision of policymakers at the institutional level using intelligent devices and knowledge that maximizes the fit between individuals and machines (e.g., Kumar et al., 2021). Another way is better analyzing the environment of public organizations using HMII and translating this analysis into business advantages that minimizes expenses for governance. The relationship may also work in the counter direction where BI supports the development and integration of HMII strategies and devices in governance, and by so doing improves the interfaces between digital technology and individuals (public employees, policymakers, and citizens). Business Intelligence strategies may thus help improve HMII by providing better insights on the way humans (employees, citizens, other stakeholders) interact with machines, their difficulties and expectations in such interactions, and the ways to overcome such barriers. Hence, if any significant policy direction (e.g., in healthcare, education, welfare or homeland security) will consider both BI and HMII elements, the public interest will benefit.

Next, we expect that HMII will be positively related with SI. Highly intelligent social environments in public spheres may significantly contribute to better HMII through the process of mutual learning. HMII may be advanced only thorough better knowing how to deal with others and how to adapt to social situations and to the emotions of individuals operating within groups in public spheres. The interaction of intelligent machine (and intelligent machine interfaces) with humans has potential significant meaning for social environments in which both machines and individuals operate. We expect that those individuals expressing high interpersonal intelligence in connecting with other humans will also be those that know better how to develop highly intelligent HMI strategies and technologies. As such, they will contribute to improving HMII, and also help in learning how to use them better. Similarly, a relationship in the counter direction may work as well. Those highly intelligent HMI strategies and interfaces may help in furnishing more intelligent social environments. They encourage individuals to become socially and emotionally wiser by learning form others (including from machines themselves), being sensitive to other individuals' views and behaviors. This can be gained by adapting to new social norms in the presence of machines and various digital governance elements, by improved regulations, and by flexible codes of behavior that deem required by others in such spheres (Wirtz et al., 2019). Moreover, when intelligent machines are integrated in governance for better management and wiser policies, the social environment of these organizations benefit from the flow of data and information and from the richness of digital machine intelligence. Thus, we expect that in the presence of HMII social intelligence in governance will be first challenged, and finally improved. Integrating learning computers and algorithms may better predict potential hazards in ongoing policies, and it may help decision-makers to better assess potential risks and barriers in future policies that involve larger number of stakeholders and individuals, sizeable investments, and potential risks. The social intelligence, on the other hand, may contribute to better designing those intelligently learning machines and IUIs. It can do so by employing collective knowledge, skills, and experience to train and teach the HMII systems. Such training of machines may be in the form of new artificial intelligence tools (e.g., ChatGPT, Brad). Thus, the HMII-SI relationship may as well be constructively bidirectional.

Finally, we also expect a similar bidirectional relationship between SI and BI. We argue that highly intelligent social environments in public spheres are necessary to build better business intelligence. This rational is based on Muntean et al. (2014) idea that social intelligence and business intelligence interrelate and are fundamental for policymakers. The relationship may work in the opposite direction as well. Governance that succeeds in establishing greater BI may be more open to the idea that SI among individuals is important. Thus, both SI and BI potentially interrelate in facilitating better services to citizens and improving public outcomes. For example, highly BI governance will be more likely and capable to encourage the recruitment of socially intelligent public servants, developing their skills and talent as another tool for maximizing public impact and public interests. SI may contribute to elevating BI to a higher level by using the collective interpersonal knowledge of individuals and government stakeholders to improve management of information and knowledge systems in bureaucracies. In return, this upgraded and improved handling of information and knowledge at the business level may advance social intelligence because groups and teams may use the acquired BI systems in daily decision-making and policy formation. That is, SI may benefit from BI as much as BI builds and rely on greater SI. Another example may be using extensive BI systems in public education and in school management for strengthening performance via constructive social ties among students, teachers, and parents. The opposite direction may be the advancement of BI systems in schools based on the knowledge and information accumulated from social circles such as groups of students, teachers, and parents. These may enrich understanding on how the goals of the entire school may be better achieved and linked to business/ managerial rational.

In sum, we argue that the IntelliGov model reflects how various types of intelligence interact with each other and altogether may affect governance and its policies. IntelliGov looks at HMII, BI, and SI as mutually and positively related, and as affecting the overall governance intelligence in many ways that still await to be explored. We therefore suggest P4 as follows

P4: *Social intelligence, human-machine intelligence, and business intelligence are positively related. Together with other types of intelligence (human. Institutional, artificial) they positively affect IntelliGov.*

7 IntelliGov in the Digital Age: How Technology Revolutionize Governance Intelligence

7.1 Evolving Artificial Intelligence: From Bits to Metaverse

Perhaps the greatest change in governance intelligence of our era is becoming more and more digital based. Digitization is probably the fourth transformative industrial revolution in human history (Awan, Sroufe, & Shabbaz, 2021). It is enriched with sophisticated artificial and technological innovations that together with information society platforms, dramatically alter many aspects of modern life. The rise of machines and algorithms is discussed and examined in growing number of studies that advance along philosophical discourse and more empirical research (e.g., Asgarkhani, 2007; Gil-Garcia, Dawns, & Pardo, 2017). All studies point to the major role of governments and a variety of public administrations organizations and agencies in this revolution, both as active players, as passive observers, and as intermediate bridging actors. They promote and support research and development in this arena, finance many of these initiatives, regulate their emergence and operation, and use its outcomes in a variety of fields and territories (Dunleavey et al., 2008; Coglianese & Lehr, 2017). Moreover, the artificial/digital revolution generates new power bases in society with which governance need to deal (e.g., virtual communities, crypto coins, and international networks of knowledge). On one hand, this revolution redefines old liberal and democratic rules and values, but on the other hand it also urges greater government regulations and interventions to safeguard public interests and the public good (e.g., Moore, 2019). In many ways the digital age of governance ultimately reformulates the meaning of intelligence in public spheres. It reconstructs the relationships between governments and citizens and intensifies the adoption of digital tools and technologies aimed at improving public sector performance and overall wisdom to act for the public, with the public. In that sense, knowledge by artificial tools and digital platforms becomes a crucial facilitator and driver of more intelligent governance.

Moreover, the digital age transforms the meaning of intelligence in general, and specifically the meaning and essence of IntelliGov, in ways we have never seen before. The development and use of nonhuman vehicles to acquire information and knowledge, and further improve physical and cognitive skills seems to dominate today's policies and decisions in almost every segment of governance activities. The process toward such domination advanced over decades. Artificial intelligence in governance and in public management has gone a long way since the first use of digital bits during the technological revolution of the information society in the late 1970. Today, more than four decades later, we witness straight talks about bots, robots, e-government and e-democracy, and inspiration goes as far as metaverse government (Wyld, 2010; Hudson-Smith, 2022). Endless sources of information and knowledge on the Web, combined with unimaginable ways to store and recall them anytime, anywhere, and for anyone create new types of governance, administration, and management of public spheres. In that sense, governance and public management of the third millennia is largely intelligent in the sense that it adopts, use, and advances digital tools for knowledge and decisions, more than any time before in history. To understand how we have come so far it is important to look into three major waves of change that affected the intelligent governance of our times.

7.1.1 Intelligent Governance and Public Management: Digitization in Three Waves

Intelligent governance and public management are related along three evolutionary waves: The first one in the middle 1970s, the second around the early 1990s, and the third one at the beginning of the 2000s and until our times.

The roots of change may be tracked back to the emergence of classic public management around half a century ago. In its first evolutionary wave, public management was heavily inspired by widespread global market orientations, a strong neo-liberal ideology, and greater ambition to increase performance and promote a business-like public sector (Vigoda, 2002; Raadshelders & Vigoda-Gadot, 2015; Young et al., 2020). However, many digital transformations of early days, especially during the late 1970s and 1980s, were premature and perceived suspiciously as unsustainable, unrealistic, or simply too hard to adopt (Katsonis & Botros, 2015). Nonetheless, this first wave of digitization allowed extension of knowledge and information in new ways that were never available before. In fact, these were the seeds of a much greater change in the coming years and the first step toward new types of intelligence in governance. The intellectual avenues of NPM and businesslike governance paved the way to greater openness, growing creativity, adaptation of technological innovations, long-range planning, extensive entrepreneurship spirit, and far-reaching modernization that allowed the rise of networks digitization as a second wave of public management revolution, and the artificial machine digitization as a third wave of transformation.

First wave: Governance through advanced public management was the beginning of intelligent governance in the digital era. It evolved dramatically since the mid-1970s with liberal thinking about better managed governance that should build on open channels of knowledge and information, especially in relation with the business sector. Similarly, better performing governance based on wiser management ideas has become the holy grail of markets and consumerism. Moving from conservative public management to New Public Management, Post-NPM, co-production and co-creation governance, and New (public) Governance (e.g., Osborne & Gaebler, 1992; McMullin, 2021), we have witnessed continues change and progress in research and practice with critical meaning to all modern nations (Vigoda-Gadot, 2009; Raadschelders & Vigoda-Gadot, 2015). The rise of public management in the late 1970s later resulted with the emergence of digitized government or the e-governance era (Dunleavy et al., 2005; Katsonis & Botros, 2015). The first wave was therefore ideological by nature, but lacking much of the reliable technological tools that became available only around two decades later. Katsonis and Botros (2015) pointed to the interest in e-government in the 1990s as occurred during the era of NPM. NPM's major principles focused on managerialism, decentralization, debureaucratization, downsizing government, privatization, and outsourcing, with the hope that they will elevate public administration and policy into a better level of performance and service delivery (Osborne & Gaebler, 1992; Vigoda-Gadot & Mizrahi, 2014). These principles were strongly rooted in economic rationalism, strive for public agencies' effectiveness, efficiency, economy, and overall performance. Principles underpinning the NPM included contestability in the delivery of public goods and services, and a shift from inputs to outputs with greater attention to performance indicators (Gahan, 2007). Digitization was a perfect fit to those ideas. It allowed a bridge between eutopia and reality with technology as a facilitator of vision.

Second wave: During the early 1990s, and alongside flourishing NPM ideas and practices, internet tools and information applications entered the government arena. Whereas the first wave was ideological by nature, the second one was largely initiated by rapid technological changes, the inventions of personal computers and mobile technologies, and the rise of the open society and open data platforms. Katsonis and Botros (2015) pointed to the interest in e-government in the 1990s as occurred during the era of NPM. Information and communication technology (ICT) was rapidly evolving and reached maturity in terms of the markets. It was intensively used as a vehicle to better efficiency, reduction of costs and public expenses, and greater accountability and productivity. Work processes benefitted from ICT and led to modern human resource management, new and inspiring ways to improve quality of services, and finally also to the emergence of 'e-government'. According to the OECD (2003, 2009), e-government was defined as having online internet services and activities, the use of ICTs in government, and the capacity to transform public administration using ICTs, but mostly with static and uni-directional internet technology (e.g., websites and emails). These 'read-only web' technology enabled the basics of electronic communication and dissemination of information with very little user interaction or content contribution (Aghaei et al., 2012). This stage was also defined as the Web 1.0 generation. Thus, e-government significantly contributed to governance intelligence but did not achieve the expected outcomes given its limited interactive capability (Katsonis & Botros, 2015). Furthermore, its impact on individuals was not systematically studied and explanatory models on the way digitization affects human mentality, knowledge, emotions, attitudes, behaviors, and values was still scarce at that stage. Whereas technology and digitization advanced rapidly, interfaces with human intelligence were only slowly progressing and overall governance intelligence remained lagging behind. Similarly, extending our knowledge on intelligent governance was also limited and only made its first steps.

Third wave: Public management and governance of the late 1990s and early 2000s opened the gate to a third wave of digitization with new ideas on public reforms and social progress (Dunleavy et al., 2005; Katsonis & Botros, 2015). The third wave came with increasing maturity of social media technologies, new tools and strategies of big data accumulation, and both hardware and software developments that allowed greater storage and faster use of information. All these are crucial for intelligent humans and nonhuman systems. With such capacities, government and governance had the chance to become wiser, smarter, and overall better than ever before in history simply due to huge amounts of information and knowledge that could now be used to maximize the public interest. Moreover, mobile technology became available to almost every individual in every point on the globe. They accelerated the spread of all types of information and knowledge and allowed intelligence to be transferred and shared in zero-time slots. The information society has now been equipped with highly sophisticated information technology (IT) which boosted the expansion of mass media and social media tools and infrastructure. The result was an unimaginative reality of bots, robots, and algorithms that entered daily lives of almost every individual on earth. Since that time, these changes also play growing role in public policy formation, assimilation, and delivery.

Greater sophistication of computer-based and mobile technologies further redefined citizens and governance relations. Together with fast adjusting human skills to such capacities, machines were also thought to better adapt to humans in many public services. Consequently, intelligence around governance was infused by ideological change among policymakers and other key stakeholders in and around public organizations. These greater openness of minds allowed entrance of machines and new-age algorithms into daily work of public servants. Larger number of open information platforms (e.g., emails, social media, large files exchange, bigger capacity of memories, sophistication of hardware and software platforms) allowed faster and more extensive transfer of data, sharing of ideas, innovations and skills, and extension of knowledge and experiences at all levels of government. Consequently, since the early 2000s we have witnessed rapid transition from human-based intelligence in governance to artificial machine-based intelligence. Public management was also enriched with new human–machine interaction (HMI) style of governance intelligence. Studies suggested that if intelligence is related with new knowledge, the centers of knowledge have started to shift from humans to machines and algorithms, from individuals to computers, and especially to the interfaces that relate them. This transition was accompanied by a variety of dilemmas such as questions of strategic development in governance and in public administration (when and in what form to use the new tools of intelligence and HMI interfaces), practice (how to use these tools), and ethics (what may be the moral impact of using such tools). Overall, it seemed that the fields of governance, public administration, and public management struggled with growing challenges and barriers to co-creation and innovation that called for even more intelligent solutions (Torfing et al., 2021).

The rise of machines such as bots, robots, and algorithms in the first two decades of the twenty-first century is at the heart of the third wave of digital transition that lasts even today. Machines based on high-technology within governance use big-public-data and multisource information systems gradually penetrate the public sector and dramatically change governance and nonprofit sector activity in many ways. Katsonis and Botros (2015: 43) describe it as "a corresponding shift from e-government to Government 2.0 with the application of Web 2.0 tools and principles to the public sector and public management." The third wave of digitization in governance uses Web 2.0 technologies which became more dynamic and socially oriented. It allows people to collaborate and share information online through tools such as blogs, wikis, RSS feeds, tagging, and other social media and social networking platforms. It enables read-write properties and harnessed the collective intelligence of users in sites such as Wikipedia, Flickr, and YouTube (O'Reilly, 2005). Government 2.0 also pave the way to greater direct citizen engagement in governments decisions and services and more extensive and authentic participation in public policy and co-production activities, also known as e-democracy. In that regard, greater collective intelligence is encouraged and promotes the public interests. Simultaneously, greater pressures for open access to public sector information and data emerged. Public sector values of collaboration, transparency, openness, and authentic engagement of both service receivers and service providers in governments decisions and actions was brought to the forefront of public deliberation. Digitization, information, data, and machines in the forms of bots, robots, and algorithms dramatically changed the way government interacted with the community, shared information, and achieved better outcomes for citizens (Victorian Government, 2010). Nevertheless, although this stage undoubtedly affected individuals in many ways, empirical research about the relationship between artificial intelligence of the third wave of digitization, and intelligent governance as a generic theme remained scarce.

Our times and the next waves: Today, the intelligence of governance calls for reconstruction and redefinition of theoretical borders, and for reevaluation of concepts, antecedents, and impacts of what we define as IntelliGov. Governance is increasingly built up on machine power. Artificial intelligence by machines is involved in almost every segment of public activity and together with human intelligence have growing impact on policies, management and overall procedures and processes in governance. Robots are part of daily routines in healthcare and in public hospitals services; cameras and sensors are spread in urban spaces, across communities and along transportation lines; biometric systems monitor borders, data and finance transaction with governance; algorithms control education, welfare, culture and environmental initiatives; community safety and communication channels are daily assessed and evaluated by governance computers and tracking systems. Only recently we were introduced with tools of artificial intelligence like ChatGPT and Bard that allow both public institutions and individuals to build skills and infrastructures of knowledge that are beyond anything produced independently before by either humans or machines. These capacities have major implication for future overall governance intelligence. They may be used to help policymakers in deciding better (e.g., Giest, 2017); they may assist bureaucrats (and street-level bureaucrats) in providing better services (e.g., Considine et al., 2022); they may extend the control and auditing circles and allow better supervision of governments outputs (e.g., Hunt et al., 2021); and they may take the lead in interacting with citizens and other stakeholders (e.g., Criado & Villodre, 2021). One of the fields that is leading these processes is national security and defense, where artificial and digital intelligent systems are intensively replacing humans in a variety of missions related with homeland security and military actions in land, marine, and air combat zones (e.g., Horowitz, 2020; Gomez & Whyte, 2021). Artificial intelligence is also increasingly used in diplomacy and foreign affair tasks (e.g., Adler-Nissen & Drieschova, 2019), healthcare, education, welfare services, and other public services. Overall, we witness exponential growth of artificial and digital intelligence infusion into our public life, beyond our personal lives. The integration of machines like bots, robots, and algorithms in all fields of governance responsibility undoubtedly contribute to their intelligence, but the potential of integrating it with human and institutional intelligence is still far from complete and may be the challenge of next waves. This integration is at the core of improving the quality of decisions and policies, improving responsiveness and services to citizens, and better using governments budgets and resources in new and open spheres. Nonetheless, maximizing the full intellectual potential of machines and algorithms still rests in improved integration among major players: People, machines, and institutional bureaucracies. This may be done largely by greater public management intelligence, by smarter tools and better knowledge that is accessible and easily adopted by individuals in daily management of public agencies.

7.1.2 IntelliGov during Crises and the Digital Age

Katsonis and Botros (2015) suggest that the one of the major facilitators of digital and artificial intelligence in governance was the global financial and economic crisis of 2008. It was the beginning of a more advanced digitization age in public management. Other crises that followed, and especially the global COVID-19 pandemic, escalated this process dramatically. Economies were heavily affected by these crises and greater citizens' expectations from government emerged. It enabled the penetration of sophisticated IT and AI into the public sphere, despite its limitations and hazards. The flow of data and information thus set higher standards for governance who was urged to become more intelligent and make better use of public resources. Citizens expected to transact with government 24/7 and thus governments became more heavily depended on digital technology for both individuals and organizations in their day-to-day activities. Studies stressed the need to improve understanding of the interfaces between machines, individuals, and the overall administrative system. Intelligent governance became more and more dependent on high-speed broadbands, advanced mobile phone technologies, cloud computing and storage of government databases, and remote accessing and processing of big data. These technologies are only some innovations that increase efficiency, speed, and responsiveness in public management of our times. However, at the same time, they also expose citizens, public organizations, and many government agencies to threats such as cyber-attacks and privacy risks never known before. Intelligence in governance is therefore advanced but also exposed to new threats of greater magnitude and scales.

The most recent illumination of the impact of digitization on intelligent governance, on citizens and on public organizations emerged during early 2020. Almost out of nowhere, the COVID-19 pandemic erupted and highlighted major dilemmas in public management and in modern governance policies. Moreover, it is already obvious today that major drawbacks in public management theories and knowledge have affected and intensified the global coronavirus pandemic crisis (e.g., Young, Wiley, & Searing, 2020; Vigoda-Gadot et al., 2023b). Examples include the miscalculation of the potential risks and lack of strategic plans for dealing with epic crises, the underestimation of the threats to democracy and governance in turbulent times and during a digital revolution of new and fake news, the incorrect preparations of policymakers and lack of international coordination and collaboration, and the overall cognitive bias in managerial decisions before and during the battle for public health. It became clear that the interactions between governments and citizens is essential to minimize damage in lives of millions and the health of even larger numbers of individuals. Digital governance turned to be a major tool for dealing with some of these problems and a vehicle to intelligent governance during crises. Digital tools, IT, algorithms, and machines offered indispensable mechanism for prevention and treatments, tracking the progress of the pandemic, assessing its impact, and taking real-time policy decisions. New technologies greatly affected governments policies and were crucial in changing individuals' attitudes and behaviors. Governance intelligence benefited from all these.

Intelligent governance today is a necessity, especially in face of broad realization that future acute crises at a global scale are only a matter of time. Thus, governance is expected to use external service providers to extend the flow of information and data between private, not-for-profit, and public agencies. These are important during crises but also in peaceful times. Mobile devices such as smartphones and tablets transform the way services are provided and accepted by end users and will undoubtedly be crucial in times of crises. They bring the demand for responsiveness and performance to higher levels and redefine public values such as greater engagement, transparency, and accountability. All these is no less important for governance in peaceful times. Take teaching in universities and academic institutions as an example. Only few years ago talks and information delivered in class were not subject to students' examination against reliable (and less reliable) web sources, at least until class ends. In today classes, anything mentioned by anyone is subject to immediate cross-check, criticism, and extension. Intelligence is thus continuously challenged by anyone, anytime, anywhere. Social media enabled transaction of knowledge and information between citizens as clients and increased new forms of citizenship, involvement. Individuals' attitudes and behaviors such as participation and engagement (Vigoda-Gadot, Shohat, & Eldor, 2013), collaboration, awareness and innovation were affected by these changes. With the expansion of online services by mega-firms such as Google, Apple, and Facebook big data sources were created and used for various purposes. Some of them promoted constructive public values, and some have threatened them significantly. But overall, crowed intelligence became part of governance intelligence. Later, during the COVID-19 pandemic in 2020 and onward it was evident that these datasets can serve the public interest well but also may potentially endanger privacy, freedom of speech, autonomy, and other democratic values.

Furthermore, Katsonis and Botros (2015) also explain how data and technological revolution resulted with flattered organizational structures that helped coping with the needs for efficiency, effectiveness, and minimizing public spending. Digital governance is a source for greater intelligence but also the result of such changes. The footprints of digital governance represented modernization strategies aimed at creating public value (OECD, 2014, 2020). The OECD found in its 2009 study that the focus on technology alone in the era of e-government overshadowed the need for organizational, governance, and cultural changes in the public sector (OECD, 2009). Various stakeholders such as government agencies, civil servants, citizens as individuals or as part of voluntary and community organizations, non-governmental agencies, the private and the finance sector are all part of this transition. Digital governance may thus support the creation of more intelligence in governance but to do so it must involve multiple delivery channels with a two-way relationship between the government and citizen. Digital, and more intelligent governance in turbulent and in peaceful times enable a whole-of-government approach compared to the singular nature of E-government.

Hence, the digital governance approach builds on several pillars that may altogether be relevant for future developments of IntelliGov as well: (1) A shift from a citizen-centric to a citizen-driven model of government services; (2) A 'digital-by-default' policy where governments make digital services the default channel for service delivery; (3) Extended use of mobile devices to access government information and services; (4) Developing new governance arrangements with more collaborative and networked systems; (6) Building the capability of the public sector through development of digital skills based on collaboration and innovation; (7) Adopting an agile approach to the design, procurement, and development of IT systems across systems and organizations; (8) Ongoing open provision of government information with appropriate security and privacy protocols; (9) Enabling a data-driven process for collecting and analyzing information about government services to inform policy development and priorities. These pillars, suggested by Katsonis and Botros (2015) are still relevant today. But are all these enough for building more intelligent governance? Nevertheless, does this process represents an evolution or revolution in intelligent governance?

7.1.3 The Power of Machines in Governance: From Evolution to Revolution?

Recently, Rona-Tas (2020: 905) suggests that algorithmic governance is "the replacement of social institutions and processes with algorithmic decision making." In that sense, one may argue that digital machines are taking over humans in forming and altering governance, its missions, data, tools, and outcomes. Novel ideas of governments by virtual reality and metaverse inspired theoretical and empirical studies throughout the years. They further promoted practical innovations in smart cities and other parts of government. However, even at this stage, integrative empirical studies on the use of modern technology and its contribution to intelligent governance suggest that we are still far from a situation of machine monopoly. Algorithms and computers cannot fully replace human intelligence and human component are still crucial in the process of public goods definition, redefinition, and delivery. Social cues, narratives, values, norms, and psychological perspectives are constantly 'folded' into governments and markets in various forms (Muniesa, 2007). Their impact on the collective and integrative governance intelligence remains indispensable.

Empirical evidence exists today as to the constructive power of technology, and the impact of digitization on performance, efficiency, service quality, and overall intelligence in governance. But studies also point to the problems and dilemmas it poses, such as interface problems, ethical issues, and the cost of adaptation and readaptation (e.g., Dunleavey et al., 2005, 2008). Moreover, digital platforms and IT innovations are expected not only to affect people and organizations but also to change norms and values related with our democratic and liberal societies. All these are inherent parts of intelligent governance. When machines become increasingly involved in the process of public goods production and public service provision, the interface between individuals, machine and organizations turn more crucial than ever. Can digital machines affect what the public need as much as they affect what it wants? Can they shape not only knowledge and skills but also aspirations and inspirations of citizens and governance? To answer these questions, we need much better interdisciplinary knowledge and understanding. Integration of digital machines and data systems in governments similarly calls for growing need to investigate the human and institutional side of interacting with machines. Our evolutionary model of IntelliGov, that was described and rationalized in the early sections of this Element explain and advocate this argument. It implies that individuals and societies need to understand, accept, and willingly adapt the new digital technology vocabulary and learn how to work with digital governance transformations. Organizations need to be receptive of digitization and make the best use of it for the public interest through their greater intelligence. To do so, human-machine-organization interfaces become essential and critical.

One of the main impacts of digital machines on individuals is in the form of attitudinal, perceptual, and behavioral changes. When artificial intelligence and digitization in public organizations results with attitudinal and behavioral changes among individuals, it may further redefine democratic and public values and boost intelligent decision-making among policymakers. For example, public values like participation, engagement, communitarianism, and good citizenship are changing vis-à-vis digital infrastructures and tools such as social media, mobile technologies, and rapid global data exchange between governmental agencies and between other partners. They allow more voice and activism of individuals and better capacities to create effective interest groups and collective pressure on governments to initiate reforms, change policies and strategies. E-democracy is thus also related with intelligent governance. The creation of networks and the collective action in and around public organization increases public impact on governance and vice-versa. The entire democratic ethos in modern states may thus take the shape of more spontaneous and authentic discourse but also with greater sensitivity and flexible nature. This may be typical of future intelligent governance frameworks.

Paradigmatically, the positivist behavioral approach in politics and government further accelerate this process (e.g., Lynn, 1996; Grimmelikhuijsen et al., 2017). This approach devoted considerable effort to theories, methodologies, and analytical frameworks aimed at better understanding individual's attitudes and behaviors in public environments. When the third wave of digitization and artificial intelligence meets a positivistic approach, greater interest is expressed in how digital machines alter our views and behaviors in relation with public services, public goods, and policy decisions in central and in local government, within communities, and across social spheres. In that sense they build intelligent tools and interfaces based on more robust empirical designs and data. These serve the public interest and the process of governing as decisions may be grounded on stronger empirical evidence. Conjoining the behavioral approach in public management with the idea of digital public management and intelligent governance is therefore a promising progress path for advancing modern nations that are based on intelligent governance. Digital and intelligent governance walks hand in hand with behavioral public administration to explain central and local government processes, decisions, and impact on citizens wellbeing. This is where intelligent Human–Machine Interactions (HMI) meets public management and governance, and questions on the interface between digital machines, humans, and public institutions become more relevant than ever. Theories on such interactions call for extension and improvement. They are essential not just from the technological and engineering perspective (e.g., a focus on what makes these interactions better, smoother, and more effective) but also from the social and administrative perspective (e.g., why, how, and when such interactions make a difference for individuals and organizations? Can they explain public organizational outcomes and individuals' reaction? Do they matter for improving public policies and enhancing public performance in goods and services?).

Moreover, as the digital evolution turns to be a full-scale revolution it is expected to foster a more intelligent governance that is committed to equal, humanized, advanced, and public-value oriented policies. To meet such goals, we must use behavioral knowledge, methodologies, and experience and integrate them with digital machines, algorithms, and information bases that are digitally controlled and monitored. Theories of "good governance" (e.g., Kaufmann & Lafarre, 2021), "new public governance" and the "co-production of services" (e.g., Sorrentino, Sicilia, & Howlett, 2018) will have to adjust by balancing the human-institution-machine impacts and the interactions between them as a major key for better public performance.

7.2 IntelliGov as an Integration of Minds

Undoubtedly, the most imminent construct of IntelliGov of recent decades builds on artificial-technological-digital capacities that dramatically increase the flow and use of data and information across public sector and governing spheres. We maintain that comprehensive intelligence in governance must rely on integration of the human, institutional, and machinery minds. The mind of machines, while integrated with human minds and with institutional minds is a powerful factor in our public environment. In that sense, AI and digitization in governance and in public management has contributed immensely to IntelliGov. It liberated the human minds to allow contributions from nonhuman minds. It emerged alongside technological revolutions and promoted new ideas and better types of intelligent governance. Such models, in forms such as good governance, smart cities, or collaborative administration are much in line with IntelliGov. Although the extent and depth of digital transformations in public sectors lag far behind the technological developments (Giest, 2017), it is clear that all nations, developed and developing, put the goal of better using information and knowledge at the forefront of their public policies. Hence, IntelliGov in its full capacity and scope may be delayed but will eventually be sustained.

The obstacles on the way are many. Citizens still face immense difficulties in handling new digital tools, and many of them are suspicious about governments' use of information and data, especially during crises and emergencies. It is also not clear how exactly the digital and AI revolution may affect the effectiveness of individuals such as public servants, the performance of public organizations as bureaucratic bodies, and the relations between governments and citizens. In the presence of digital transformation in governance and in public management, social relations among all parties who are involved in production and consumption of public goods and services take new shapes and nature. Resulting from them are new and serious problems at both the individual, institutional and overall policy levels (e.g., increased inequality, lower mobility, corruption, differentiation is service delivery and outreach, changing nature of public jobs: e.g., Bastida et al., 2021; Roberts et al., 2020). Furthermore, studies in public administration and management tend to suggest general, often philosophical, analyses of these processes, or alternatively focus on very specific aspects of the dilemmas in ways that leave much space for more integrative and multi-level models for intelligent governance to grow and flourish.

Nevertheless, digital transformation and AI is a major addition to IntelliGov and adds enormously to more traditional pillars of human and institutional intelligence. Its centrality will intensify with the years as it develops faster than any other element in the model. Its impact on our lives dramatically increases, not only with natural technological advancement but also due to the fact that people everywhere become dependent in those digital technologies and machinery wisdom. This dependency is highlighted during external events and emergencies such as the global economic crisis of 2008 and the eruption of the COVID-19 pandemic (Dunleavey et al., 2005, 2008; Shen et al., 2023), and other global crises such as international armed conflicts, the global terror threat, and environmental climate change hazards (Clark & Albris, 2020). Greater digitization extensively affects public policies and strategies, and fast translated into managerial practices at the organizational and street levels. Crises and emergencies such as the COVID-19 global pandemic exemplified how digital platforms in the hands of governments were used to deal with healthcare concerns. In some countries this battle was managed and won with more intelligence and less damage. But in other countries, with much less intelligence, the outcomes were much worse. In all countries, however, it became evident that advanced digital technologies such as AI also created quite troubling problems related with privacy, human rights, citizens' trust, and other impacts on democratic values (e.g., Cheng et al., 2020; Mizrahi et al., 2021; Vigoda-Gadot et al., 2023a, 2023b). We thus argue that in such circumstances of governance in turbulent times, better interactions of humans, machines, and institutions is critical for building more intelligent governance. The road toward turning this into reality is still long. Thus, the idea of IntelliGov in the technological-digital age deserves more attention and a systematic look. The next section deals with these future challenges.

8 Future Studies on Intelligent Governance: Major Challenges

What we have tried to demonstrate so far is that intelligence in governance may worth exploration and construction as a stand-alone phenomenon. So far, this idea as a concept, field of study, variable or even a measure is largely underdeveloped. To be acknowledged as a valuable theoretical and empirical idea it needs to add scholarly value which is beyond what we already know about intelligence in general. Its value should be recognized based on aggregation and integration of interdisciplinary knowledge. Intelligent governance may be seen as a puzzle of pieces with close, but far from identical, concepts, jargons, terminologies, scales, and measures. To infuse the meaning of intelligence governance with critical scientific mass scholars should clearly identify these pieces and deal with several types of challenges resulting from the creation of the new puzzle. Table 1 suggests a short review of these major challenges that may help unveil the meaning of Intelligent Governance in the digital era. It includes theoretical, methodological, and analytical challenges that altogether may open gates to new streams of studies with better understanding of the public sphere, and by employing an interdisciplinary, multi-level, and multi/mixed-method perspectives. The table illustrates how complex intelligence governance may be, and how we can foster better knowledge in this field in the coming years.

8.1 Theoretical Challenges

The theoretical challenges for the study of intelligent governance are many, and they stand at the forefront of our concern and capability to defend this idea as an autonomous scholarly territory. Such challenges include epistemological, conceptual, exploratory, and explanatory problems. The most prominent theoretical challenge is *epistemological*, that is, well defining the sources of knowledge that are essential for the creation of intelligent governance as an abstractive and

Table 1 Major challenges for the study of Intelligent Governance (IntelliGov)

	Challenge		Focus	Major question
1. Theoretical	Epistemological		Deep meaning of what intelligence means for Governance and other public agencies	What is the meaning of IntelliGov?
		Conceptual	Clear Distinction among close terminologies (e.g., talent, skills, knowledge, wisdom, smart, good, new, advanced)	How is it different from other concepts?
		Exploratory	Unpacking the meaning of concepts by rich information aggregated in previous studies across disciplines	What do we already know based on past knowledge?
		Explanatory	Mapping core relationships in the literature and pointing to major evidence already supported in past studies (using SLR – Systematic Literature Reviews, and theoretical meta-analysis).	Which variables may be useful for the study of IntelliGov?
2. Methodological	Measurement issues		Clarifying what we measure; Suggesting testable measures. Confirming validity and reliability of scales at various levels of analysis (individual, group, institutional/organizational, artificial).	How to measure IntelliGov?

	Research designs and samples	Developing potential experimental, quasi-experimental, and non-experimental designs; defining potential samples and respondents among governance stakeholders	How to study IntelliGov?
	Strategies for intervention	Developing better strategies to acquire data; identifying potential methodological barriers; mapping suitable qualitative and quantitative methods for the study of intelligence; Using Mixed-Methods approach.	How to conduct field intervention for IntelliGov?
3. Analytical	Soft-qualitative analysis	Testing appropriate qualitative methods in the field; Employing qualitative statistical tools for human, institutional and artificial intelligence	What the stories about IntelliGov tell us? How to interpret them?
	Hard-empirical analysis: Using Multi-level and Multi/mixed methods	Testing appropriate quantitative methods in the field; Employing advanced quantitative statistical techniques for human, institutional and artificial intelligence; Suggesting mix method analysis to combine knowledge on intelligence from human, institutional and artificial sources. Using Big-Data sources to redefine questions and hypotheses.	What are the core variables that empirically relate with IntelliGov? Why do they matter? When? And for whom?

functional idea. These sources of knowledge should be as rich as possible and may even include, at first stage, philosophical, ideological, linguistic, and even normative thoughts about the epistemic nature of IntelliGov across settings, times, cultures, populations, and cultures. This should help in convincing the scientific community about the importance of intelligent governance for global knowledge. Such knowledge undoubtedly rests on interdisciplinary knowledge of the social science, but further on the humanistic, natural, environmental, and life sciences. More specifically, epistemological considerations should stimulate thinking in public administration, public management, public policy, and governance.

Stemming from the epistemological challenges are *conceptual* concerns. Studies are encouraged to identify a set of related concepts, rooted in different worlds of knowledge, that may later help understand intelligence in governance, its antecedents, and outcomes. The conceptual challenge should strive to portray clearer borders for what intelligence in government really means and to advance consensus among researchers about its internal and external validity. For example, how concepts like knowledge, information, skills, and talent relate with intelligence. Can we make clear distinction between them and the various facets of intelligence in governance (e.g., human and nonhuman, rational and motional, business and institutional, social and artificial)? These conceptual frameworks may also give rise to additional terminologies that are unknown or unrecognized today as valuable enough for the study of IntelliGov. They can result from extensive mapping of the thematic building blocks of multiple intelligence in governance.

After major epistemological and conceptual challenges are met, even partially, another level of progress should be the *exploratory* one. At this stage theoretical exploration of relevant ideas related with the concepts identified earlier is needed. Scholars engaged at exploratory efforts will most likely disagree about how much concepts such as learning and deep learning, information and data, knowledge and understanding, problem-solving skills and improvisation combine together to build up a cohesive scholarly platform of IntelliGov. An even more demanding task would be to relate these, and other concepts and ideas, to the capacities of bureaucracies and governance to better perform at various cultures, under different sets of values, and across time and changing environmental events (e.g., peaceful times, emergencies, political crises, social disorder, and economic decline). The exploratory challenge is thus important for building a map of both existing knowledge and future potential of extended knowledge related with the theoretical frameworks for intelligent governance. This will set the ground for the final theoretical challenge which is more explanatory.

Finally, the *explanatory* challenge is the most prominent and complicated among all. How intelligent governance affect policies and management of public institutions and can it bring better outcomes for the benefit of nations and the citizens. Specific models that may explain such outcome variable should be designed and tested empirically with a search for prominent variables at various levels (e.g., individual, institutional, digital, global). The behavioral approach in public administration may contribute immensely at this stage focusing on experimental models and robust direct and indirect explanations for IntelliGov and its essence. The models may also look for the major ante-cedents that may advance intelligent governance in different ways, across socio-political environments and under local, regional, national, federal, and global restraints. The explanatory challenge will allow portraying the specific direc-tions, magnitudes, and forms of relationships. It may lead to determining if and how intelligent governance affects the performance of bureaucracies and the resulted wellbeing and prosperity of our communities. It may be also possible to suggest direct and indirect aspects of the relationships across various types of governance settings and sectors (government ministries, not-for-profit organ-izations, service agencies, public firms, civic-society institutions).

8.2 Methodological Challenges

The methodological challenges resulting from the theoretical ones are several. They include measurement issues and considerations of validity and reliability threats, problems of appropriate research designs, complexity of human and nonhuman samples, and strategies for intervention within governance and around it.

The *measurement issues* relate with building appropriate scales (for humans), instruments (for nonhumans), and other research tools to measure types of intelligent in governance and IntelliGov as whole. Measurements can be sub-jective (e.g., individuals' report their views, attitudes, predispositions, percep-tions, behavior intentions, and actual behaviors) or objective (third parties like managers, citizens, or external stakeholders report their views and assessments of others). These may include use of psychological and psychometric measure-ments, as well as economical, fiscal, judicial, and other objective archive data that is beyond attitudinal and behavioral data. Alongside this process proper assurance of validity and reliability for the proposed scales should be guaran-teed. Another challenge will be integrating the new types of measurements and scales into a coherent multilevel framework that gives a better picture of the nature of IntelliGov. Due to its multilevel and interdisciplinary nature, this measurement challenge is complex and will undoubtedly result in additional questions that to date have not even arisen.

The challenge of constructing appropriate *research designs and samples* must first consider the distinction between experimental and non-experimental designs. Within the framework of experimental (and quasi-experimental) designs studies on intelligent governance should well define the level of analysis of intelligence. For human intelligence in governance studies will most likely seek samples of individuals working for governance and around it (public servants, street-level bureaucrats, citizens, decision-makers, etc.) while for nonhuman intelligence in governance the focus will be on institutional and organizational units, as well as on digital machines and computerized systems (e.g., bots, robots, algorithms, AI systems). Designs will need to consider the distinction of general individual intelligence from collective institutional intelligence and ways to assess them objectively in comparative models. The study in each one of these directions will call for specific definition and adjustment of measurements and scales to the research targets. A resulting question will obviously be the integration of knowledge from the human and the nonhuman type of studies on intelligence into a lucid body of knowledge on IntelliGov. Research designs will need to conduct multilevel analyses of individual and nonindividual measures as well.

Finally, future studies will have to deal with *strategies for intervention within governance and around it.* These strategies can take an objective and neutral approach toward examination of multiple levels of intelligence in governance, with minimal risks of errors such as common-method and common-source bias. Interventions are likely to be formed in the shape of employing different levels of analysis such as (1) individuals or groups/teams, (2) units within organizations, (3) institutions as a whole, via senior policy/decision-makers or through documentation, archives, or other data sources, (4) artificial platforms and technologically based information sources such as video-audio channels and other types of sensors. Ethical issues will apparently be relevant and involved at considering each one of these levels. Strategies for intervention and analyzing intelligence should also promote mixed-methods techniques for integrating knowledge among all levels of analysis. These may cover, for example (1) collecting bias-free data on IntelliGov at the individual/human level and on IntelliGov at the institutional and artificial levels, (2) developing useful ways to use more objective information about intelligence in governance against more subjective information, (3) integrating digital technology-based data sources (e.g., brain scanning by fMRI, physical tests and biological/clinical/physical indicators) into more human-based data sources (e.g., surveys, observations, simulations, experiments) and distinguishing more clearly when exactly these are useful and testable, and (4) usefully combining all these sources of data into larger data-bases on the whole-of-IntelliGov.

8.3 Analytical Challenges

Among the analytical considerations related to studies on IntelliGov one can point to two major potential directions. Studies that adopt more soft-qualitative analysis methods will most likely need to resolve issues related with exploration and deep learning of specific cases, comparative problems of looking beyond specific cultures and traditions, and mapping the accumulated knowledge about interdisciplinary aspects of governance intelligence. The alternative direction of hard-empirical analysis methods will need to deal with analyzing well defined and established measures that are testable, re-constructable, objective, and falsifiable. Within this direction a major challenge will be finding suitable settings to test the theoretical ideas, defining the appropriate levels of analysis, and getting data from humans and digital machines in a way that also builds effective interfaces to ensure successful bridge of the digital gap.

The *soft-qualitative analysis* method track is necessary for better understanding the meaning of intelligence among various stakeholders, and its interpretation at the artificial-digital-technical level. Soft-qualitative methods such as Systematic Literature Reviews, Qualitative Comparative Analysis and qualitative meta-analyses, strategies for mapping knowledge with Network Analysis are extremely useful to provide a road map for the extension of knowledge on how intelligence can master decisions and lead to better policymaking, policy formation, and policy implementation. Comparative tools may provide useful cases of how intelligence is used (or misused) in governance across agencies, tasks, and services. Systematic comparative analysis may also track steps for turning governance and individuals within government organizations into more intelligent players in the way the produce knowledge, information, and insights based on reliable data for the benefit of citizens. Comparative studies that also integrate the use of digital systems, data and big-data sources with policy decisions are useful from a cultural perspective as well. Studies acknowledge today that the digital interface works differently across nations and cultures (Kinn Abass, 2021). It is largely affected by value-based perceptions and attitudes as individuals differ in their interpretations of information around them. Thus, various stakeholders in and around governing bodies use different presumption, dispositions, experience, and beliefs about governance when they act and respond to relevant public problems. They develop "digital trust," alongside traditional trust in governance decisions and actions, and comparative studies should aim at learning this process in detail.

The *hard-empirical analysis* method track follows the soft-qualitative stage to provide more objective replicable data on this phenomenon, its transition, development, and relationship with antecedents and outcomes. The hard-empirical methods will undoubtedly make use of the full range of options embedded in the behavioral/ cognitive sciences, natural/neurosciences, computer science, political science, public administration, and governance. These may vary from interviews to surveys, comparative methods, experiments (natural, surveys, and lab), observations, and simulations (Vigoda-Gadot & Vashdi, 2020). No doubt that each of these methods has much to offer to better understanding IntelliGov. Structured, semi-structured, and open interviews with different stakeholders may explore variants of intelligence in public spheres to which we have not yet been exposed or aware. Surveys may contribute extensive knowledge on individuals' attitudes, perceptions and emotions related with IntelliGov. These may reflect rational and emotional reactions to knowledge generation and assimilation in public agencies and around them. One question that may be relevant is how various aspects of intelligence in governance may affect each other and if the entire IntelliGov structure is the simple sum of all intelligent capacities around governance, or alternatively, it is much more than that? Only quantitative empirical analyses may reveal some answers in these directions. In addition, empirical and analytical challenges also include integration of multilevel and multi/mixed-method approaches. Analyses from neuroscience and computer science of IntelliGov should be integrated with more social and behavioral/cognitive analyses in useful ways. This may advance creation and use of Big-Data sources with social, economic, clinical, and artificial data all within one data setting. It may than allow redefinition of original questions and hypotheses about IntelliGov. As intelligent governance has roots in personal, social, institutional, and digital level analysis, new approaches should seek ways to integrate them usefully. Thus, collaboration between scientists from various fields such psychology, cognitive sciences, sociology, political science, organizational and business studies, economy, computer science and engineering is crucial.

9 Discussion: Toward a Theory of Multiple Intelligence in Governance

In the previous sections, we gradually developed the idea that intelligence is a prominent and relevant concept for governance and that it should be studied more thoroughly, considering its multiple forms, levels of analysis, and heterogeneous perspectives. We proclaimed that governance can be intelligent, but that to become such several challenges should be met. These include more persuasive and holistic theories, innovative and integrative models, and adequate methodological and empirical strategies to bridge them. Starting from the seminal studies on human intelligence of the early twentieth century (e.g., Binet, 1916; Terman & Merill, 1937; Piaget, 1972), moving through the understanding that there might be multiple types of intelligence (e.g., Gardner, 1983; Salovey & Mayer, 1990;

Herrnstein & Murray, 1994; Woolley et al., 2010), and until our digital-age times of artificial intelligence, E-governance, and E-democracy (e.g., Adams, 2004; Glikson & Woolley, 2020), the intelligence of governance still awaits comprehensive scholarly attention. The relatively few studies that tried to deal with governance intelligence have done so from quiet limited and narrow perspectives (e.g., EI, or AI, or II in governance) but none so far has come up with an integrative approach in the interdisciplinary way proposed here.

This Element suggests that an advance on this road may benefit from an integrative and interdisciplinary view of various approaches to the study of intelligence in the context of public institutions, public administration and management, bureaucracies, public stakeholders, and the evolving technological revolution. The comprehensive interdisciplinary model for intelligent governance (IntteliGov) demonstrates how all previous evolutionary stages can be combined into one solid framework. Thus, Figure 5 and Table 2 provide a broader examination of the comprehensive IntteliGov model by

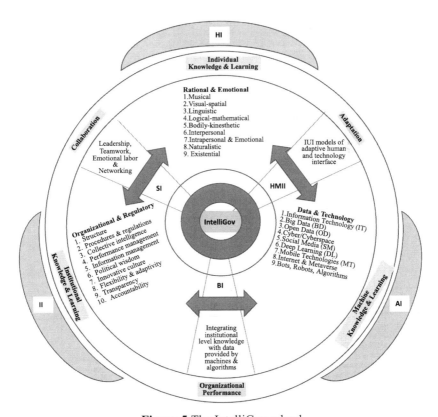

Figure 5 The IntelliGov wheel

Table 2 Intelligent Governance (IntelliGov): An interdisciplinary multiple intelligence perspective and potential scientific contribution

	HI	II	AI	HMII	SI	BI	Intelligent Governance (IntelliGov)
Discipline	Behavioral science, neuroscience	Management, political science, public administration & policy	Computer science and Data science	Engineering, natural and exact science, behavioral science	Social science, sociology, communication, Cognitive science	Business organizations, information systems	Interdisciplinarity
Level of analysis	Individual	Institutional	Machine	Human-Machine	Individual-Institutional	Institution-Machine	Governance: individuals, institutions, policies, and machines
Definition	Mental and emotional ability to reason, plan, solve problems, think abstractly, comprehend complex ideas, learn quickly, and learn from experience, and interact with others	Capability of an institution/ organization to comprehend and create knowledge relevant to their goals and markets	The talent we relate to computers, algorithms, and other machines in our environment to use data, handle it, and use it to solve complex problems	Those systems that provide tools to help minimize the cognitive distance between the mental model that the user has of the task and the way in which the task is presented to the user by the computer when the task is performed	Capacity to deal with people and social relationships.	Strategies and technologies used by enterprises for the data analysis and management of business information.	Integration of HI, II, AI, SI, HMII, & BI for better public management and policy in and around governing institutions

Potential Contribution: Theoretical and applied						
Theoretical: Better understanding how intelligence among public stakeholders (policymakers, bureaucrats, SLBs, citizens) develops and evolves, and how it relates with governance performance	Theoretical: Better understanding how intelligence of public organizations, bureaucracies, and related agencies develops and evolves and how it relates with governance performance.	Theoretical: Better understanding on how machines in service of governance acquire intelligence and how they support human behavior and the performance of governance.	Theoretical: Better understanding on how humans and machines interact intelligently. Explaining the role of IUI interfaces in advancing public performance and the public interest.	Theoretical: Better understanding of how individuals interact intelligently and collectively work for governance. Develop explanations for the role of social intelligence in enhancing IntelliGov.	Theoretical: Better understanding how institutional intelligence use information and knowledge provided by machines in governance, to support and advance public goals. How BI in governance is formed and how it affects public performance and the public interest.	Theoretical: Better understanding how intelligence in governance is formed and changes, what makes an impact on its evolvement over time, across cultures, organizations, and digital environments.
Applied: Improving public servants' intelligence using knowledge & learning models and maximizing their impact on governance performance	Applied: Improving public organizations collective intelligence using knowledge & learning models and maximizing their impact on governance performance	Applied: Improving machine learning capacities of managing information and knowledge and maximizing their impact on governance performance	Applied: Improving adaptation of AI to HI with intelligent interfaces that continuously learn and adopt to public interests	Applied: Improving collaboration among intelligent public servants and creating collective public value	Applied: Developing practical tools and methods to advance integration of institutional knowledge & learning with machine knowledge and information, for better public outcomes.	Applied: developing tools and methods for the measurement and improvement of policies and management in governance to maximize performance and public interest.

Table 2 (cont.)

	HI	II	AI	HMII	SI	BI	Intelligent Governance (IntelliGov)
Suggested research questions	1. How civil servants' intelligence evolves? 2. Can citizens intelligence contribute to better government decisions and how? 3. Mapping the role of multiple HI types in the context of IntelliGov. 4. How to measure public stakeholders' intelligence in the context of governance?	1. What makes an impact on II? 2. Exploring the constructs of II in governance. 3. What is the contribution of II to public performance? 4. How to measure II in the context of governance?	1. What is the impact of AI on IntelliGov? 2. Are some AI tools more relevant to governance than other? In what way? 3. Does AI work differently in different nations/culture types of governance? How? 4. What encourages more effective use of AI in governance?	1. What is a better HMII for governance? 2. How HMII mediate the HI-II impact on public outcomes? 3. What are constructive and destructive impacts of HMII on policies? 4. How to compare the effectiveness of HMII in governance across cultures and nations?	1. What are the facets of SI in governance? 2. How to measure SI in governance? 3. Do individuals working for government need special SI skills and knowledge? and what? 4. How SI affects IntelliGov?	1. Is BI different in governance as compared with other organizations? 2. What type of BI is ideal for governance? 3. What is the impact of BI on governance performance? 4. How to measure BI in governance?	1. How to assess IntelliGov? 2. What types of intelligence more important for IntelliGov? 3. Does culture affects IntelliGov? How? 4. What makes a difference among Nations in their IntelliGov? 5. What is the impact of IntelliGov on performance? 6. Does IntelliGov matters in forming more democratic values? How?

Threats to	Intelligence			
	Mentally biased decision-making and emotional driven decisions that are less rational, more intuitive, and thus unfit with facts and detached from reality.	lack of organizational training to teams, ill skills of public managers, and unprofessional political effects that may endanger the capacity of bureaucracies to use knowledge and talents competently and thus to damage policy outcomes	Low quality and low reliability of machine technology and computerized algorithms, insufficient and wrong information and data that may cause wrong machine discretion, and insensitive HMI interfaces that will limit access of various populations to public services.	-

illustration of (1) the IntteliGov Wheel and, (2) a comparative assessment of intelligence constructs for governance.

The IntelliGov wheel is presented in Figure 1. It details a series of internal facets within each type of intelligence, as suggested in the relevant literature of the discipline in which they were developed. The contribution of the IntteliGov wheel is threefold. First, it suggests a fuller interdisciplinary perspective on the types of intelligence that may be relevant for governance, with closer attention to variants within each type. Second, it portrays the links among all types of intelligence and highlight interconnections that can be further developed, rationalized, and empirically tested in future studies. Finally, it looks at the better and more effective type of intelligent governance as equally benefited from human, institution, machine learning, and the knowledge aggregated and used in a collective manner. The IntelliGov idea aims at inspiring thinking on advanced learning tools and methods to secure expansion and assimilation of reliable knowledge at all levels of governance. This may advance sustainable progress of public policies and public management to meet the public interest over time, with intelligence as a pillar of mental models, strategies, and long-range evolution. It illustrates how intelligent governance involves human, institutional, and artificial skills to support better bureaucratic decisions and greater governability, under democratic values of freedom of mind and collective trust. It is aimed at higher service quality, effectiveness, and efficiency of governing agencies, and, simultaneously, advancing social virtues of fairness, equity, and resilience within these agencies and around them. The IntteliGov wheel offers better resolution of interconnections between facets of each type of intelligence and allows a more inclusive perspective. Both the comprehensive IntelliGov model and the IntelliGov wheel exemplify how various types of intelligence at all levels and by all sources, integrate and have special meaning for governance. We believe that such a comprehensive perspective on intelligence in governance may elevate public administration and other public agencies to a higher level of learning, understanding, adopting, and developing knowledge for public goals and in service of the collective public interests.

To help in summarizing our ideas, Table 2 suggests a comparative look into the conceptual and theoretical foundations for IntelliGov. According to this table, different human, institutional, social, business, and digital inputs should be assessed and developed in several ways. First, the *disciplinarity origins* of each type of intelligence should be recognized and acknowledged. Effort is needed to bridge the disciplinary gaps which also determine the *level of analysis* for intelligent governance. A major challenge in this direction is creating interdisciplinary thinking of models that combine the various perspectives and bridge them theoretically, methodologically, empirically, and practically. Moreover, it is also essential to define the potential *theoretical and applied contributions* of each field of knowledge about intelligence. We tried to suggest several such directions, but we are well aware that other directions may rise and evolve with time. Consequently, we more specifically postulated several *research questions* to expand knowledge on each type of intelligence, in relation with the comprehensive IntteliGov model. For example (1) How to assess IntelliGov? (2) What types of intelligence more important for IntelliGov? (3) Does culture affect IntelliGov? How? (4) What makes a difference among Nations in their IntelliGov? (5) What is the impact of IntelliGov on governance performance? (6) Does IntelliGov matters in forming more democratic values? How?

Finally, it may also be worth mentioning the major potential threats to IntelliGov. These include threats at the individual, institutional and artificial levels. At the individual level major threats are mentally biased decision-making and emotional driven decisions that are less rational, more intuitive, and thus unfit with facts and detached from reality. At the institutional level the IntelliGov model may suffer from lack of organizational training of teams, ill skills of public managers, and unprofessional political effects that may endanger the capacity of bureaucracies to use knowledge and talents competently and thus to damage policy outcomes. At the technological level the IntelliGov model may be endangered by low quality and low reliability of digital machine technology and computerized algorithms, insufficient and wrong information, and miscalculated data that may cause wrong digital machine discretion. These may also result with insensitive HMI interfaces that will limit access of various populations to public services. These potential threats to the development of intelligent governance should be carefully examined and considered in future studies.

10 Summary: Can Governance Be Intelligent, and How?

This theoretical manuscript tried to gradually develop an inclusive agenda and a set of evolutionary models for the study of intelligence in governance. We presented constructs of intelligence as suggested in the rich literature that evolved over more than a century. Its roots are in psychology, but it had fast grown to affect various disciplines as well. The greatest challenge for scholars in political science, governance, public administration, and public management and policy is to make sense of integrating them into a sound analytical framework. Hence, the uniqueness and potential contribution of this Element is in setting the ground for more interest in governance as intelligent entities and doing so in a way that may inspire future theory and empirical efforts. We believe that by applying human, institutional, and artificial/machine knowledge and tools, intelligent governance can become a field worth of explicit study and development. Understanding it theoretically may drive applied knowledge as well, which may help policymakers, public managers, and street-level bureaucrats make more informed and effective decisions. These will further improve the delivery of services to citizens and increase efficiency and transparency in government operations.

Good/wise/smart/sound and intelligent governance of our times heavily rely on modern public management which has evolved as a unique interdisciplinary field of knowledge within other disciplines. These include, but not limited to, political science, public administration, public policy, management, organizational behavior, economy, and many other social and behavioral disciplines. However, its digital and technological orientation is quite new and belongs to recent decades only. In its classic aspiration, classic public management used marketplace ideology and neo-liberal ideas to try and transform conservative public administration into a new type of governance that better suits the modern age of consumerism, individualism, capitalism, and business-like ideologies. In that sense, it may be argued that public management encouraged intelligence in governance. It profoundly and ideologically justified the use of vast knowledge and tools in a process of redefining the expectations from governance. In many ways it posed the goal of intelligent governance as a necessity of modern-liberal nations. Recent years' technological advancements in the fields of computers, information systems, machines such as bots, robots, and algorithms, as well as mass (social) media and communication, dramatically transform public management and governance (e.g., Liva et al., 2020), and thus also challenge its intelligence.

Thus, intelligence in governance as well has moved from its human based knowledge to more sophisticated digital machine and human-machine sphere. IT and digitization in governance became an integral part of our lives as citizens and public customers. Digitization became a buzz word in public management and its impact today on public organizations, government agencies, citizens, civic servants, and policymakers, as well as other stakeholders in the public arena is undisputable. Theoretically, it redefined our expectations, aspirations, and exchange relations with governments and its agents. Similarly, we expect governance to be more intelligent than ever, and when it fails to meet higher standards, we criticize it and increase demands. Practically, the new forms of intellect and the rise of big-data and extensive knowledge-based policies, brought question of intelligent governance to our front door. Such intelligence is undoubtedly affected by our rising levels of knowledge, greater skills, and growing experience, but even more so by our attitudes, perceptions, and behaviors in relation to governance decisions and actions. These also give birth to new models of intelligence development by integrating machines, humans, and their interfaces in public service.

Future challenges for studying IntelliGov are thus many, and we suggest only a partial list: (1) Establish the construct validation of measurements for intelligence in governance, at the individual, social/organizational and digital levels. (2) examine the possibility for generic intelligence in governance, across sectors, agencies, cultures, and traditions; (3) explore the evolution of IntelliGov by better understanding the roots, formation, and development over time and cases; (4) analyze the different stages of intelligence formation in government; (5) Map the major barriers that obscure governments from becoming more intelligent, and specifying differences between more and less intelligent governments using comparative methods; (6) Develop concrete field studies to test public administration as an intelligent workplace; (7) Test how problem solving, and policy decisions are affected by intelligent governance; (8) Practically improve intelligence in governance based on the theoretical knowledge

We hope that such directions for future research may yield innovative models with improved explanatory power for the meaning of intelligence in governing halls, and for how governments can work better for citizens. We believe that the idea of intelligent governance may significantly change our view of public organizations theory and practice, contributing to the public interests. It may become a promising path to increase citizens' welfare and prosperity while minimizing inequalities and ills caused by natural or man-made social threats, and by blunders of policymakers.

References

Adams, N. B. (2004). Digital intelligence fostered by technology. *Journal of Technology Studies, 30*, 93–97.

Adler-Nissen, R., and Drieschova, A. (2019). Track-change diplomacy: Technology, affordances, and the practice of international negotiations. *International Studies Quarterly, 63*, 531–545.

Aghaei, S., Nematbakhsh, M., and Farsan, H. (2012). Evolution of the world wide web: From web 1.0 to Web 4.0. *International Journal of Web and Semantic Technology, 3*, 1–10.

Apperly, I. A., and Butterfill, S. A. (2009). Do humans have two systems to track beliefs and belief-like states? *Psychological Review, 116*, 953–970.

Asgarkhani, A. (2007). Digital government and its effectiveness in public management reforms: A local government perspective. *Public Management Review, 7*, 465–487.

Awan, U., Sroufe, R., and Shahbaz, M. (2021). Industry 4.0 and the circular economy: A literature review and recommendations for future research. *Business Strategy and the Environment, 30*, 2038–2060.

Baron-Cohen, S. (1991). Precursors to a theory of mind: Understanding attention in others. In A. Whiten (ed.), *Natural Theories of Mind: Evolution, Development, and Simulation of Everyday Mindreading* (pp. 233–251). Cambridge, MA: B. Blackwell.

Bastida, F., Estrada, L., and Nurunnabi, M. (2021). Empirical determinants of corruption in Honduran municipalities. *Public Integrity, 24*(7), 629–643. https://doi.org/10.1080/10999922.2021.1958561.

Berman, E. M., and West, J. P. (2008). Managing Emotional Intelligence In US Cities: A Study Of Social Skills Among Public Managers. *Public Administration Review, 68*(4), 742–758.

Binet, A. (1916a) [1905]. New methods for the diagnosis of the intellectual level of subnormals. In E. S. Kite (trans.), *The Development of Intelligence in Children: The Binet-Simon Scale* (pp. 37–90). Baltimore: Williams & Wilkins.

Binet. A., and Simon, T. (1916). *The Development of Intelligence in Children.* Baltimore: Williams & Wilkins. (Reprinted 1973, New York: Arno Press; 1983, Salem, NH: Ayer Company).

Bloom, H. 2000. *Global Brain: The Evolution of Mass Mind From the Big Bang to the 21st Century.* John Wiley & Sons, Ne

Brunetto Y., Teo S. T., Shacklock, K., and Wharton, R. F. (2012). Emotional Intelligence, Job Satisfaction, Well-Being And Engagement: Explaining

Organisational Commitment And Turnover Intentions In Policing. *Human Resource Management Journal*, *22*(4), 428–441.

Bullock, J. B. (2019). Artificial Intelligence, Discretion, and Bureaucracy. *The American Review of Public Administration*, *49*(7), 751–761.

Carrigan, C., and Coglianese, C. (2011). The politics of regulation: From new institutionalism to new governance. *Annual Review of Political Science*, *14*, 107–129.

Cheng, Y., Yu, J., Shen, Y., and Huang, B. (2020). Coproducing responses to COVID-19 with community-based organizations: Lessons from Zhejiang province, China. *Public Administration Review*, *80*, 866–873.

Choo, C. W. (1998). *The Knowing Organization: How Organizations Use Information to Construct Meaning, Create Knowledge, and Make Decisions.* Oxford: Oxford University Press.

Ciarrochi, J., Forgas, J. P., and Mayer, J. D. (2001). *Emotional Intelligence In Everyday Life: A Scientific Inquiry.* New York, NY: Psychology Press.

Clark, N., and Albris, K. (2020). In the Interest(s) of Many: Governing Data in Crises. *Politics and Governance*, *8*(4), 421–431.

Coglianese, C., and Lehr, D. (2017). Regulating by robot: Administrative decision making in the machine-learning era. *Georgetown Law Journal*, *105*, 1147–1223.

Considine, M., Mcgann, M., Ball, S., and Nguyen, P. (2022). Can robots understand welfare? Exploring machine bureaucracies in welfare-to-work. *Journal of Social Policy*, *51*, 519–534.

Coren, S. (1995). *The Intelligence of Dogs.* New York: Bantam Books.

Criado, J. I., and Villodre, J. (2021). Delivering public services through social media in European local governments: An interpretative framework using semantic algorithms. *Local Government Studies*, *47*, 253–275.

Crozier, M. (2008). Listening, learning, steering: New governance, communication and interactive policy formation. *Policy & Politics*, *36*, 3–19.

Cukurova, M., Luckin, R., and Kent, C. (2020). Impact of an artificial intelligence research frame on the perceived credibility of educational research evidence. *International Journal of Artificial Intelligence in Education*, *30*, 205–235.

Detterman, D. K., and Sternberg, R. J. (eds.) (1982). *How and How Much Can Intelligence Be Increased?* Mahwah: Erlbaum.

de Sousa, W. G., de Melo, E. R. P., De Souza Bermejo, P. H., Farias, R. A. S., and Gomes, A. O. (2019). How and where is artificial intelligence in the public sector going? A literature review and research agenda. *Government Information Quarterly*, *36*, 101392.

Dunleavy, P., Margetts, H., Bastow, S., and Tinkler, J. (2005). New public management is dead. Long live digital-era governance. *Journal of Public Administration Research and Theory*, *16*, 467–494.

Dunleavy, P., Margetts, H., Dunleavy, P., Bastow, S., and Tinkler, J. (2008). *Digital Era Governance: IT Corporations, the State, and E-government.* Oxford: Oxford University Press.

Eshuis, J., de Boer, N., and Klijn, E. H. (2023). Street-level bureaucrats' emotional intelligence and its relation with their performance. *Public Administration, 101*(3), 804–821. https://doi.org/10.1111/padm.12841.

Gahan, P. (2007). The politics of partnership. In M. Pittard and P. Weeks (eds.), *Public Sector Employment in the Twenty-first Century* (pp. 229–254). Canberra: ANU.

Gardner, H. (1983). *Frames of Mind: The Theory of Multiple Intelligences.* New York: Basic Books.

Giest, S. (2017). Big data for policymaking: Fad or fast track? *Policy Sciences, 50,* 367–382.

Gilad, B., and Gilad, T. (1986). SMR forum: Business intelligence. The quiet revolution. *Sloan Management Review, 27,* 53–61.

Gil-Garcia, J. R., Dawes, S. S., and Pardo, T. A. (2017). Digital government and public management research: Finding the crossroads. *Public Management Review, 17,* 633–646.

Glikson, E., and Woolley, A. W. (2020). Human trust in artificial intelligence: Review of empirical research. *Annals, 14,* 627–660.

Glynn, M. A. (1996). Innovative genius: A framework for relating individual intelligences to innovation. *The Academy of Management Review, 21*(4), 1081–1111.

Goleman, D. (2006). *Social Intelligence: The New Science of Human Relationships.* New York: Bantam Books.

Gomez, M. A., and Whyte, C. (2021). Breaking the myth of cyber doom: Securitization and normalization of novel threats. *International Studies Quarterly, 65,* 1137–1150.

Gonçalves, A. G., Kolski, C., de Oliveira, K. M., Travassos, G. H., and Grislin-Le Strugeon, E. (2019). A systematic literature review on intelligent user interfaces: Preliminary results. In Adjunct Proceedings of the 31st Conference on l'Interaction Homme-Machine (IHM '19 Adjunct) (pp. 1-8). New York: Association for Computing Machinery, Article 5.

Gottfredson, L. S. (1997). Mainstream science on intelligence (editorial). *Intelligence, 24,* 13–23.

Gottfredson, L. S. (1998). The general intelligence factor. *Scientific American Presents, 9,* 24–29.

Grimmelikhuijsen, S., Jilke, S., Olsen, A. L., and Tummers, L. (2017). Behavioural public administration: Combining insights from public administration and psychology. *Public Administration Review, 77,* 45–56.

Grossi, G., Meijer, A., and Sargiacomo, M. (2020). A public management perspective on smart cities: "Urban auditing" for management, governance and accountability. *Public Management Review*, *22*, 633–647.

Guy, M. E., and Lee, H. J. (2015). How Emotional Intelligence Mediates Emotional Labor In Public Service Jobs. *Review Of Public Personnel Administration*, *35*(3), 261–277.

Guy, M. E., Newman, M. A., and Mastracci, S. H. (2008). *Emotional Labor: Putting The Service In Public Service*. Armonk, NY: M.E. Sharpe, Inc.

Hancock, P.A, & Chignell, M.H. (Eds.). (1989). *Intelligent Interfaces: Theory, research, and design*. Amsterdam: North-Holland

Heath, S. B. (1983). *Ways with words*. New York: Cambridge University Press

Hedlund, J. (2020). Practical intelligence. In R. Sternberg (ed.), *The Cambridge Handbook of Intelligence* (Cambridge Handbooks in Psychology, pp. 736–755). Cambridge: Cambridge University Press.

Henman, P. (2020) Improving public services using artificial intelligence: possibilities, pitfalls, governance. *Asia Pacific Journal of Public Administration*, *42*(4), 209–221.

Hsieh, C. W. (2009). *Emotional Labor In Public Service Roles: A Model Of Dramaturgical And Dispositional Approaches* (Doctoral Dissertation). The Florida State University.

Herrnstein, R. J., and Murray, C. (1994). The *Bell Curve: Intelligence and Class Structure in American Life*. New York: Free Press.

Horowitz, M. C. (2020). Do emerging military technologies matter for international politics? *Annual Review of Political Science*, *23*, 385–400.

Hudson-Smith, A. (2022). Incoming metaverses: Digital mirrors for urban planning. *Urban Planning*, *7*, 343–354.

Hunt, T. (1928). The measurement of social intelligence. *Journal of Applied Psychology*, *12*, 317–334.

Hunt, J. O. S., Rosser, D. M., and Rowe, S. P. (2021). Using machine learning to predict auditor switches: How the likelihood of switching affects audit quality among non-switching clients. *Journal of Accounting and Public Policy*, *40*, 1–17. https://doi.org/10.1016/j.jaccpubpol.2020.106785.

Jaquero, L., Montero, F., Molina, J. P., and Gonzalez, P. (2009). Intelligent user interfaces: Past, present and future. In R. Miguel, B. Crescencio, and O. Manuel (eds.), *Engineering the User Interface* (pp. 1–12). London: Springer.

Janssen, M., Brous, P., Estevez, E., Barbosa, L. S., and Janowski, T. (2020). Data governance: Organizing data for trustworthy Artificial Intelligence. *Government Information Quarterly*, *37*, 1–8.

Joseph, D. L., and Newman, D. A. (2010). Emotional Intelligence: An Integrative Meta-Analysis And Cascading Model. *Journal Of Applied Psychology, 95*(1), 54–78.

Katsonis, M., and Botros, A. (2015). Digital government: A primer and professional perspectives. *Australian Journal of Public Administration, 74,* 42–52.

Kaufmann, W., and Lafarre, A. (2021). Does good governance mean better corporate social performance? A comparative study of OECD countries. *International Public Management Journal, 24,* 762–791.

Kinn Abass, B. (2021). Culture and digital divide influence on e-government success of developing countries: A literature review. *Journal of Theoretical and Applied Information Technology, 98,* 1362–1378.

Kittur, A., Lee, B., and Kraut, R. E. (2009). Coordination in collective intelligence: The role of team structure and task interdependence. In *CHI 2009: Proceedings of the ACM 27th International Conference on Human Factors in Computing Systems* (pp. 1495–1504). New York: ACM Press.

Kohler, W. (1925). *The Mentality of Apes.* E. Winter (trans.), 2nd ed. London: Kegan Paul, Trench, Trubner. U.S. edition 1925 by Harcourt: Brace & World.

Kolski, C., and Le Strugeon, E. (1998). A review of intelligent human-machine interfaces in the light of the ARCH Model. *International Journal of Human–Computer Interaction, 10,* 193–231.

Kotzé, M., and Venter, I. (2011). Differences in emotional intelligence between effective and ineffective leaders in the public sector: An empirical study. *International Review of Administrative Sciences, 77,* 397–427.

Kristof, K., Andrew, R. A., and Conway, A. (2019). Unified cognitive/differential approach to human intelligence: Implications for IQ Testing. *Journal of Applied Research in Memory and Cognition, 8,* 255–272.

Kumar, S., Raut, R. D., Queiroz, M. M., and Narkhede, B. E. (2021). Mapping the barriers of AI implementations in the public distribution system: The Indian experience. *Technology in Society, 67,* 1–9. https://doi.org/10.1016/j.techsoc.2021.101737.

Lavee, E., Cohen, N., Nouman, H. (2018). Reinforcing public responsibility? Influences and practices in street-level bureaucrats' engagement in policy design. *Public Administration, 96,* 333–348.

Law, K. S., Wong, C. S., and Song, L. J. (2004). The construct and criterion validity of emotional intelligence and its potential utility for management studies. *Journal of Applied Psychology, 89*(3), 483–496.

Legg, S., and Hutter, M. H. (2007a). A collection of definitions of intelligence. *Advances in Artificial General Intelligence: Concepts, Architectures and Algorithms, 157,* 17–24.

Legg, S., and Hutter, M. H. (2007b). Universal intelligence: A definition of machine intelligence. *Minds and Machines*, *17*, 391–444.

Levitats, Z., and Vigoda-Gadot, E. (2017). Yours, emotionally: How emotions infuse motivation for public service and job outcomes of public personnel. *Public Administration*, *95*, 759–775.

Levitats, Z., and Vigoda-Gadot, E. (2020). Emotionally engaged civil servants: Towards a multi-level theory and multi-source analysis in public administration. *Review of Public Personnel Administration*, *40*, 426–446.

Levitats, Z., Vigoda-Gadot, E., and Vashdi, R. D. (2019). Engage them through emotions: Exploring the role of emotional intelligence in public-sector engagement. *Public Administration Review*, *79*, 841–852.

Liva, G., Codagnone, C., Misuraca, G., Gineikyte, V., and Barcevicius, E. (2020). Exploring digital government transformation: A literature review. *Proceedings of the 13th International Conference on Theory and Practice of Electronic Governance (ICEGOV 2020)*. New York. 502–509.

Lynn, L. E. (1996). *Public Management*. New Jersey: Chatham House.

March, J. (1999). *The Pursuit of Organizational Intelligence*. Oxford: Blackwell.

March, J. G., and Olsen, J. P. (1984). The new institutionalism: Organizational factors in political life. *American Political Science Review*, *78*, 734–749.

Mayer, J. D., and Salovey, P. (1997). What Is Emotional Intelligence? In P. Salovey and D. Sluyter (eds.), *Emotional Development And Emotional Intelligence: Implications For Educators* (pp. 3–31). New York: Basic Books.

McManus, S., Seville, E., Vargo, J., and Brunsdon, D. (2008). Facilitated process for improving organizational resilience. *Natural Hazards Review*, *9*, 81–90.

McMaster, M. D. (1996). *The Intelligence Advantage: Organizing for Complexity*. Newton: Butterworth-Heinemann.

McMullin, C. (2021). Challenging the necessity of new public governance: Co-production by third sector organizations under different models of public management. *Public Administration*, *99*, 5–22.

Meijer, A., and Bolívar, M. P. R. (2016). Governing the smart city: A review of the literature on smart urban governance. *International Review of Administrative Sciences*, *82*, 392–408.

Mikalef, P., Lemmer, K., Schaefer, C., et al. (2022). Enabling AI capabilities in government agencies: A study of determinants for European municipalities. *Government Information Quarterly*, *39*(4). https://doi.org/10.1016/j.giq.2021.101596.

Mizrahi, S., Vigoda-Gadot, E., and Cohen, N. (2021). How well do they manage a crisis? The government's effectiveness during the COVID-19 Pandemic. *Public Administration Review*, *81*, 1120–1130.

Moore, S. (2019). Digital government, public participation and service transformation: The impact of virtual courts. *Policy & Politics, 47*, 495–509.

Muniesa, F. (2007). Market technologies and the pragmatics of prices. *Economy and Society, 36*, 377–395.

Munoz, J. M. (2018). *Global Business Intelligence*. New York: Routledge.

Muntean, M., Cabău, L.G., and Rînciog, V. (2014). Social business intelligence: A new perspective for decision makers. *Procedia – Social and Behavioral Sciences, 124*, 562–567.

Neisser, U., Boodoo, G., Bouchard, T. J. et al. (1996). Intelligence: Knowns and unknowns. *American Psychologist, 51*, 77–101.

OECD (2003). *The E-government Imperative*. Paris: OECD.

OECD (2009). *Rethinking E-government Services: User Centred Approaches*. Paris: OECD.

OECD (2014). *Recommendation of the Council on Digital Government Strategies*. Paris: OECD.

OECD (2020). Digital Government Index: 2019 results, *OECD Public Governance Policy Papers*, No. 03, Paris: OECD.

O'Reilly, T. (2005). What is Web 2.0? http://oreilly.com/web2/archive/what-is-web-20.html (last accessed March 28, 2023).

Osborne, D., and Gaebler, T. (1992). *Reinventing Government*. New York: Plume.

O'Shaughnessy, M. R., Schiff, D. S., Varshney, L. R., Rozell, C. J., and Davenport, M. A. (2022). What governs attitudes toward artificial intelligence adoption and governance? *Science and Public Policy, 50*(2), 161–176. https://doi.org/10.1093/scipol/scac056.

Ostrom, E. (1990). *Governing the Commons: The Evolution of Institutions for Collective Action*. Cambridge: Cambridge University Press.

Ott, D. L., and Michailova, S. (2018). Cultural intelligence: A review and new research avenues. *International Journal of Management Reviews, 20*, 99–119.

Panch, T., Pearson-Stuttard, J., Greaves, F., and Atun, R. (2019). Artificial intelligence: Opportunities and risks for public health. *The Lancet Digital Health, 1*, e13–e14.

Park, Y. J., and Jones-Jang, S. M. (2022). Surveillance, security, and AI as technological acceptance. *AI & Society, 38*, 2667–2678. https://doi.org/10.1007/s00146-021-01331-9.

Pereira, G.V., Parycek, P., Falco, E., and Kleinhans, R. (2018). Smart governance in the context of smart cities: A literature review. *Information Polity, 23*, 143–162

Piaget, J. (1972). *The Psychology of Intelligence*. Totowa: Littlefield Adams.

Raadschelders, J., and Vigoda-Gadot, E. (2015). *Global Dimensions of Public Administration and Governance: A Comparative Voyage*. California: Jossey-Bass.

Radu, R. (2021). Steering the governance of artificial intelligence: National strategies in perspective. *Policy & Society, 40*, 178–193.

Ramsden, S., Richardson, F. M., Josse, G. et al. (2011). Verbal and non-verbal intelligence changes in the teenage brain. *Nature, 479*, 113–116.

Rauhaus, B. M. (2022). Public service motivation of street-level bureaucrats amidst the COVID-19 pandemic: An analysis of experiences in implementation of an at-home vaccination program. *State and Local Government Review, 54*, 82–91.

Rensing, L., Koch, M., and Becker, A. (2009). A comparative approach to the principal mechanisms of different memory systems. *Naturwissenschaften, 96*, 1373–1384.

Roberts, J. A., and David, M. E. (2020). The social media party: Fear of missing out (FoMO), social media intensity, connection, and well-being. *International Journal of Human-Computer Interaction, 36*(4), 386–392.

Rona-Tas, A. (2020). Predicting the future: Art and algorithms. *Socio-Economic Review, 18*, 893–911.

Ross, E. (2000). *Intelligent User Interfaces: Survey and Research Directions*. Bristol: University of Bristol.

Rotberg, R. I. (2014). Good governance measures. *Governance, 27*, 511–518.

Roth G. (2015). Convergent evolution of complex brains and high intelligence. *Philosophical Transactions of the Royal Society of London B, Biological Sciences, 370*(1684), 1–9.

Saghiri, A. M., Vahidipour, S. M., Jabbarpour, M. R., Sookhak, M., and Forestiero, A. (2022). A survey of artificial intelligence challenges: Analyzing the definitions, relationships, and evolutions. *Applied Sciences, 12*, 4054. https://doi.org/10.3390/app12084054.

Salovey, P., and Mayer, J. D. (1990). Emotional Intelligence. *Imagination, Cognition and Personality, 9*, 185–211.

Sanchez, C., Cedillo, P., and Bermeo, A. (2017). A systematic mapping study for intelligent user interfaces – IUI. *Proceedings of the International Conference on Information Systems and Computer Science (INCISCOS)*, 361–368.

Schuller, B. W. (2015). Modelling user affect and sentiment in intelligent user interfaces: A tutorial overview. In *Proceedings of the 20th International Conference on Intelligent User Interfaces (IUI '15)*, 443–446. New York: Association for Computing Machinery.

Shen, Y., Cheng, D. Y., and Yu, J. (2023). From recovery resilience to transformative resilience: How digital platforms reshape public service provision during and post COVID-19. *Public Management Review, 25*(4), 710–733. https://doi.org/10.1080/14719037.2022.2033052.

Simonton, D. K. (2012). Quantifying creativity: Can measures span the spectrum? *Dialogues in Clinical Neuroscience, 14,* 100–104.

Singh, H. P., and Kumar, P. (2021). Developments in the human machine interface technologies and their applications: A review. *Journal of Medical Engineering & Technology, 45,* 552–573. https://doi.org/10.1080/03091902.2021.1936237.

Smith, G. T. (2017). *Institutional Intelligence: How to Build an Effective Organization.* Downers Grove, Il; IVP Academic

Stern, W. (1914). The psychological methods of testing intelligence. G. M. Whipple (trans.), *Educational Psychology Monographs, 13.* Baltimore: Warwick & York.

Sternberg, R. J. (1985). *Beyond IQ: A triarchic theory of human intelligence.* Cambridge University Press.

Sternberg, R. J. (2020). Rethinking what we mean by intelligence. *Phi Delta Kappan, 102*(3), 36–41.

Sternberg, R. J., and Detterman, D. K (eds.). (1986). *What is intelligence? Contemporary viewpoints on its nature and definition.* Norwood, NJ: Ablex.

Sternberg, R. J. (1989). *The Triarchic Mind: A New Theory of Human Intelligence.* Westminster: Penguin Books.

Sternberg R. J., and Salter, W. (1982). *Handbook of Human Intelligence.* Cambridge: Cambridge University Press.

Sorrentino, M., Sicilia, M., and Howlett, M. (2018). Understanding co-production as a new public governance tool. *Policy & Society, 37,* 277–293.

Taeihagh, A. (2021). Governance of artificial intelligence. *Policy and Society, 40*(2), 137–157,

Talaoui, Y., and Kohtamäki, M. (2021). 35 years of research on business intelligence process: A synthesis of a fragmented literature. *Management Research Review, 44,* 677–717.

Terman, L. M., and Merrill, M. A. (1937). *Measuring Intelligence: A Guide to the Administration of the new Revised Stanford-Binet tests of Intelligence.* Boston: Houghton Mifflin.

Torfing, J., Ferlie, E., Jukić, T., and, Ongaro, E. (2021). A theoretical framework for studying the co-creation of innovative solutions and public value. *Policy & Politics, 49,* 189–209.

Trewavas, A. (2005). Green plants as intelligent organisms. *Trends in Plant Science, 10,* 413–419.

Tsoukas, H. (2005). *Complex Knowledge: Studies in Organizational Epistemology.* Oxford: Oxford University Press.

Victorian Government (2010). *Government 2.0 Action Plan*. Melbourne: Department of Premier and Cabinet.

Vigoda-Gadot, E. (2002). From responsiveness to collaboration: Governance, citizens, and the next generation of public administration. *Public Administration Review, 62*, 515–528.

Vigoda-Gadot, E. (2007). Citizens' perceptions of organizational politics and ethics in public administration: A five-year study of their relationship to satisfaction with services, trust in governance, and voice orientations. *Journal of Public Administration Research & Theory, 17*, 285–305.

Vigoda-Gadot, E., (2009). *Building Strong Nations: Improving Governability and Public Management*. Farnham: Ashgate.

Vigoda-Gadot, E., and Meisler, G. (2010). Emotions in management and the management of emotions: The impact of emotional intelligence and organizational politics on public sector employees. *Public Administration Review, 70*, 72–86.

Vigoda-Gadot, E., and Mizrahi, S. (2014). *Managing Democracies in Turbulent Times: Trust and Citizens' Participation as a Road to Better Governance*. Berlin: Springer.

Vigoda-Gadot, E., and Vashdi, R. D. (eds.) (2020). *Handbook of Research Methods in Public Administration, Management and Policy*. Cheltenham: Edward Elgar.

Vigoda-Gadot, E., Schohat, l., and Eldor, L. (2013). Engage them to public service: Conceptualization and empirical examination of employee engagement in public administration. *American Review of Public Administration, 43*, 516–537.

Vigoda-Gadot, E., Cohen, N., and Mizrahi, S. (2023a). Battling COVID-19: How good public management relates with resilience and trust among healthcare employees during a global crisis. *Review of Public Personnel Administration, 43*(3), 583–613. https://doi.org/10.1177/0734371X221111479.

Vigoda-Gadot, E., Mizrahi, S., Cohen, N., and Mishor, E. (2023b). Citizens' reactions to global crises: A longitudinal study during the COVID-19 pandemic in Israel. *Springer Nature (SN) Social Sciences, 3*(2), 24. https://link.springer.com/article/10.1007/s43545-023-00610-0.

Virtanen, P., and Vakkuri, J. (2016). Searching for organizational intelligence in the evolution of public-sector performance management. *Journal of Public Administration and Policy, 8*, 89–99.

Vygotsky, L. S. (1978). *Mind in Society: The Development of High Psychological Processes*. Cambridge, MA: Harvard University Press.

Wahlsten, D. (2002). The theory of biological intelligence: History and a critical appraisal. In R. J. Sternberg and E. L. Grigorenko (eds.), *The General Factor of Intelligence: How General is it?* (pp. 245–277). Mahwah: Lawrence Erlbaum Associates.

Wang, G., Xie, S., and Li, X. (2024). Artificial intelligence, types of decisions, and street-level bureaucrats: Evidence from a survey experiment. *Public Management Review, 26*(1), 162–184.

Wasserman, J. D. (2018). A history of intelligence assessment: The unfinished tapestry. In D. P. Flanagan and E. M. McDonough (eds.), *Contemporary Intellectual Assessment: Theories, Tests, and Issues* (pp. 3–55). New York: The Guilford Press.

Wechsler, D. (1944). *The Measurement of Adult Intelligence.* Baltimore: Williams & Wilkin.

Wilensky, H. L. (1967). *Organizational Intelligence; Knowledge and Policy in Government and Industry.* New York: Basic Books.

Wirtz, B. W., Weyerer, J. C., and Geyer, C. (2019). Artificial intelligence and the public sector-applications and challenges. *International Journal of Public Administration, 42*, 596–615.

Wong, Chi-Sum, and Kenneth S. Law. (2002). The effects of leader and follower emotional intelligence on performance and attitude: An exploratory study. *The Leadership Quarterly, 13*(3), 243–274.

Woolley, A. W. (2011). Responses to adversarial situations and collective intelligence. *Journal of Organizational Behavior, 32*, 978–983.

Woolley, A. W., Chabris, C. F., Pentland, A., Hashmi, N., and Malone, T. (2010). Evidence for a collective intelligence factor in the performance of human groups. *Science, 330*, 686–688.

Wyld, D. C. (2010). A Second Life for organizations?: managing in the new, virtual world. *Management Research Review, 33*(6), 529–562.

Young, M. M., Bullock, J. B., and Lecy, J. D. (2019). Artificial Discretion as a Tool of Governance: A Framework for Understanding the Impact of Artificial Intelligence on Public Administration. *Perspectives on Public Management and Governance, 2*(4), 301–313.

Young, S. L., Wiley, K. K., and Searing, E. A. M. (2020). Squandered in real time: How public management theory underestimated the public administration-politics dichotomy. *American Review of Public Administration, 50*, 480–488.

Cambridge Elements ≡

Public and Nonprofit Administration

Andrew Whitford

University of Georgia

Andrew Whitford is Alexander M. Crenshaw Professor of Public Policy in the School of Public and International Affairs at the University of Georgia. His research centers on strategy and innovation in public policy and organization studies.

Robert Christensen　　　　．

Brigham Young University

Robert Christensen is professor and George Romney Research Fellow in the Marriott School at Brigham Young University. His research focuses on prosocial and antisocial behaviors and attitudes in public and nonprofit organizations.

About the Series

The foundation of this series are cutting-edge contributions on emerging topics and definitive reviews of keystone topics in public and nonprofit administration, especially those that lack longer treatment in textbook or other formats. Among keystone topics of interest for scholars and practitioners of public and nonprofit administration, it covers public management, public budgeting and finance, nonprofit studies, and the interstitial space between the public and nonprofit sectors, along with theoretical and methodological contributions, including quantitative, qualitative and mixed-methods pieces.

The Public Management Research Association

The Public Management Research Association improves public governance by advancing research on public organizations, strengthening links among interdisciplinary scholars, and furthering professional and academic opportunities in public management.

Cambridge Elements ☰

Public and Nonprofit Administration

Elements in the Series

Contingent Collaboration: When to Use Which Models for Joined-up Government
Rodney J. Scott and Eleanor R. K. Merton

The Hidden Tier of Social Services: Frontline Workers' Provision of Informal
Resources in the Public, Nonprofit, and Private Sectors
Einat Lavee

Networks in the Public Sector: A Multilevel Framework and Systematic Review
Michael D. Siciliano, Weijie Wang, Qian Hu, Alejandra Medina, and David
Krackhardt

Organizing and Institutionalizing Local Sustainability: A Design Approach
Aaron Deslatte

When Governments Lobby Governments: The Institutional Origins of
Intergovernmental Persuasion in America
Youlang Zhang

Public Administration and Democracy: The Complementarity Principle
Anthony M. Bertelli and Lindsey J. Schwartz

Redefining Development: Resolving Complex Challenges in a Global Context
2nd edition
Jessica Kritz

Experts in Government: The Deep State from Caligula to Trump and Beyond
Donald F. Kettl

New Public Governance as a Hybrid: A Critical Interpretation
Laura Cataldi

The Courts and the President: Judicial Review of Presidentially Directed Action
Charles Wise

Standing Up for Nonprofits: Advocacy on Federal, Sector-wide Issues: An Analysis
with Case Studies
Alan Abramson and Benjamin Soskis

Can Governance be Intelligent?: An Interdisciplinary Approach and Evolutionary
Modelling for Intelligent Governance in the Digital Age
Eran Vigoda-Gadot

A full series listing is available at: www.cambridge.org/EPNP

Printed in the United States
by Baker & Taylor Publisher Services